School of Divinity

Gardner-Webb University
School of Divinity

To Be Born Again

To Be Born Again

THE CONVERSION PHENOMENON

David Poling

A DOUBLEDAY-GALILEE ORIGINAL
DOUBLEDAY & COMPANY, INC.
GARDEN CITY, NEW YORK
1979

ISBN 0-385-14324-9
Library of Congress Catalog Card Number 78–20092
Copyright © 1979 by David Poling
All Rights Reserved
Printed in the United States of America
First Edition

The author and publisher gratefully acknowledge permission to quote material from the following sources:

All Scripture except where otherwise noted is from the Revised Standard Version of the Bible, copyrighted 1946, 1952, © 1971, 1973.

Abridgment from pages 23 and 25 in *A World Split Apart*, by Aleksandr I. Solzhenitsyn. Copyright © 1978 by The Russian Social Fund for Persecuted Persons and Their Families. English translation Copyright © 1978 by Harper & Row, Publishers, Inc. Reprinted by permission of Harper & Row, Inc. and The Bodley Head (published in England under the title of *Alexander Solzhenitsyn Speaks to the West*).

The Art of Becoming a Whole Person, by Cecil Osborne. Copyright © 1978 by Word, Incorporated, Waco, Texas 76703. Material from pages 42 and 104 used by permission of Word Books, Publisher, Waco, TX 76703.

Between a Rock and a Hard Place, by Mark Hatfield. Copyright © 1976 by Word, Incorporated, Waco, Texas 76703. Material from pages 212 and 217 used by permission of Word Books, Publisher, Waco, TX 76703.

Bread for the Wilderness, Wine for the Journey: The Miracle of Prayer and Meditation, by John Killinger. Copyright © 1976 by Word, Incorporated. Material from pages 11 and 12 used by permission of Word Books, Publisher, Waco, TX 76703.

The Experience of Inner Healing, by Ruth Carter Stapleton. Copyright © 1977 by Ruth Carter Stapleton. Material from pages 152 and 174 used by permission of Word Books, Publisher, Waco, TX 76703.

From Power to Peace, by Jeb Stuart Magruder. Copyright © 1978 by Jeb Stuart Magruder. Material from pages 213 and 218 used by permission of Word Books, Waco, TX 76703.

An excerpt from "Prayer" from *Solzhenitsyn: A Pictorial Record* © Editions du Seuil, 1974. English translation © 1974 by Farrar, Straus & Giroux, Inc. Reprinted with the permission of Farrar, Straus & Giroux, Inc.

"Religion Up, Morality Down," by Charles Colson. Copyright © 1978 by *Christianity Today*. Excerpt from the July 21, 1978, issue used by permission.

This book is for Jane and John Boyd who gave the author summer shelter; Mark Hatfield, who brought hope and encouragement; Lois Jackson, who gave hours of manuscript preparation; Ann Reid Poling, who asked hard theological questions in gentle ways; Alex Liepa, whose patience and persistence became a Christian virtue.

Contents

Introduction

This book is one attempt to understand the born-again events that are touching so many lives in America today. And it is apparent that people are deeply affected by the resurgence of religious conversion that has affected politicians, criminals, movie stars, and sports personalities. Recently, George Gallup, Jr., and his organization asked people in America this question:

> Would you say that you have been born again or have had a born again experience—that is, a turning point in your life when you committed yourself to Christ?

More than a third of those questioned replied in the affirmative, with nearly half of the Protestants responding yes.

The born-again experience tells us much about the spiritual climate of our North American community—it reveals a hunger for spiritual satisfaction and fulfillment. It informs us of millions of people who felt lost and distressed and turned to Christ for meaning and salvation. Believers are saying that something good, positive, and hopeful has entered their life. In his Western classic, *Wild Rivers and Mountain Trails*, Donald Ian Smith has an illustration of what we are pursuing in this book. This rancher/preacher has spent most of his life in the high

country of Idaho. He is familiar with the harsh realities of
the wilderness and the brutal consequences of getting
lost.

He suggests that whenever you plan a camping trip or
a trail ride (or even a cookout or picnic) you are also creating the risk of getting lost. This is not a moral question
or an ethical conflict—it just happens. People get turned
around, confused, end up taking the wrong trail, miss a
sign, and are surprised by dusk. Suddenly, we can be
completely and frightfully lost. Having raised a lively and
inquisitive family in the mountain West, Smith as a par-
ent recognized early the danger of lostness for his children and the terror that can paralyze a youngster in such
a predicament. So he developed "lostness drills" for his
offspring—just as public schools conduct fire drills for
their students.

Dr. Smith wanted his children to be prepared for real
danger should they ever be separated in the rugged
mountains of Idaho. His rules are worth memorizing:

1. When lost, stop wandering and wait. Make yourself as
   comfortable as possible, but stay in one place.
2. From time to time make noise by singing or rapping
   on a hollow log. Sounds and signals can carry far.
   Frequent racket can help others find you.
3. The most important teaching—"over and over we gave
   them assurance that if they were lost, because of our
   love for them, they could be sure that we would
   never give up searching until we found them. . . .
   They would need to have confidence in their father's
   love and be trusting enough to wait for him to find
   them."

These are times, surely, when every person reading this
has experienced a sense of lostness. This wilderness, without signs or directions, was not the Rockies of the West

nor the White Mountains of New Hampshire, but the jungle of our own living.

We have all had moments of shocking doubt and disabling fears. There has been emotional and spiritual breakdown that is painful, indeed. In some periods many wander from the essentials of the Christian life and drift into the seductive philosophies of a secular age.

The heart of the Christian message helps us on such wilderness sojourns—the loving Spirit of Christ, like the caring father in Idaho, never gives up the search, never tires of seeking his own. When one has found the companionship of the Christian life, survival, safety, and joy are close at hand.

Those who have received a born-again experience testify to a sensation of wholeness and a feeling of personal integration. They perceive in life fresh expectations for fulfillment, and spiritual realities unfold that had never been realized. This book is simply an attempt to relate the current events of faith to the ancient truths that pointed to this hour.

DAVID POLING

To Be Born Again

I

Born Again—Starting with the Scriptures

The personal salvation theme did not begin with Watergate nor is it reserved for the last two centuries of popular evangelism in America. The Bible highlights a great and abiding urgency for individual change, for renewal and reclamation, for a fresh expression of a new and genuine relationship with God the Father.

In his *Daedalus* article "National Trauma and Changing Religious Values," a profound essay on the staggering changes that have saturated American life in the last two decades, Sydney Ahlstrom lists five issues that severely jarred the equilibrium of people in North America: racism and civil rights, Vietnam War and imperialism, sexism and ERA, environmental concerns, and Watergate and the abuse of government power.

The result of all this public and private furor was that "never before in the country's history have so many Americans expressed revolutionary intentions and actively participated in efforts to alter the shape of American civilization in almost every imaginable aspect—from diet to diplomacy; from art to the economic order."

While this supermarket of social and political issues is impressive and heady, the most tumultuous sounds came from the arena of religion. And those topics that had political or social or economic labels were finally to reveal a deeply religious current that vitally affected individual lives.

Concluded the Yale historian: "Moral shock, the sudden discovery that dry rot has weakened the supporting members of a very comfortable structure of values, is a traumatic experience often followed by religious doubt which then yields, gradually or suddenly to a new religious and ethical outlook."

While educational institutions, political parties, and organized churches were to feel the shock waves of this new moral discomfort, especially by young people who believed that justice had been perverted and bypassed in the establishment settings, individuals were to absorb the gulps of this revelation and many came to a born-again experience right out of the New Testament. The celebrity conversions would have a vivid impact in this media–mass communications society. Some were political prisoners—sentenced by their own moral failures, such as Charles Colson and Jeb Stuart Magruder. Others were revolutionary figures, such as Eldridge Cleaver, whose rebirth to Christianity stunned communists and Black Panthers alike, but none were so startled as mainline Christians. Then there were the notorious converts: Larry Flynt, fresh from his publishing success with a pornographic magazine, and a generous assortment of cinema and sports stars such as Johnny Cash of Nashville and Craig Morton of the Denver Broncos who reached another sector of American life.

One national writer concluded that most of the born-again people are demonstrating the essence of evangelical Christianity—the honesty to admit one's problems, the humility to seek God's help, and the readiness to accept people as they are. While these are classic New Testament attributes and are certainly apparent in the lives of many notorious converts, it continues to send waves of doubt through establishment churches—and their naturally doubtful friends, especially the press. What really is the basis for a born-again believer? What are the ground rules for this phenomenon, and where are the roots in the religious tradition of Christians?

The person who has experienced the power of being born again is the first one to mention that his or her former life was frequently one of rebellion and striking self-indulgence. The discussion that I have had with many Christians who consider the before and after events that now mark their life is consistent on this point: prior to their conversion, they were following the dictates of self and selfishness. While many were not notorious "sinners," still their values, goals, and yearnings were centered on self-gratification and a firm, steady denial of God in their lives. The denial of God and the rejection of the Lordship of Christ is more often a very subtle put-down than a stark furious negation, for many church members float along on a tide of pleasant good works and minimal standards of ethical behavior without the slightest intention of bringing their hearts to the truth.

To be born of the Spirit is to have a drastic reordering of one's whole way of looking at the world and permitting Christ to have the center of that divine/human encounter.

To receive the good news is to be willing to hear the accusations of one's own heart, that is, to admit personally and consciously that we are in mortal difficulty, that our initial impulse has been away from God, and that our living arrangements have denied the need of a Savior or even the reality of sin. Satan's greatest power is complete when we say that he no longer exists.

Many within the edges of the Christian community have substituted a doctrine of good works for the need to hear the good news. R. E. C. Browne once wrote, "Ministers of the Word deny the truth of the Gospel when they equate the good news with a message about morality." Pagans can and do express many ethical values in their lives—but such expressions cannot, for Christians, be the high goal of the Christian life.

No one put it better than Robert Raines when he told his Columbus, Ohio, congregation that "the New Testament is not good taste but good news."

The great invitation is being offered over and over again. The graciousness of God comes, as St. Paul wrote, "while we were yet helpless, at the right time. . . ." (Rom. 5:6–8) And suddenly the awakened soul discovers that Christ is able to supply what is lacking, what we can never gain or achieve or produce—a forgiven, restored life to God. Christians see in the Cross the evil of the world and the sustaining love of God. In the resurrection of Easter morning, the born-again follower sees the end of the old man and the beginning of the new. An amazing new adventure has begun, for Christ not only confirmed God's presence in his life and ministry, his death and resurrection, but offers this release from sin and death to every believer. His Christmas present to us arrives on Easter—the gift of eternal life and the welcoming into that life now.

To be born again is to be personally aware of a new citizenship, a new passport, new entry papers that proclaim the reality of a joyous, triumphant kingdom. As Hans Küng put it so elegantly in *On Being A Christian,*

> The kingdom of God is come for all and the requirements of repentance, of a new way of thinking, of a new attitude to life, of doing God's will, of love, forgiveness, service, renunciation are in principle the same for all. And this alone is the decisive factor.

The need for moral change and the necessity for personality alteration saturates the Scriptures. The personal salvation theme did not begin with Watergate nor is it reserved for the last two centuries of popular evangelism in America. The Bible highlights a great and abiding urgency for individual change, for renewal and reclamation, for a fresh expression of a new and genuine relationship with God the Father.

While the history of the patriarchs (Abraham, Isaac, and Jacob) predates the arrival of Moses, none of these "who walked with God" were to have the impact or influence of the great lawgiver from Mount Sinai. Moses was able to understand the holiness of God in worship and the justice of God in the lives of his people. But more —he experienced a personal link with Almighty God—so close that

> when Moses came down from Mount Sinai, with the two tablets of the testimony in his hand as he came down from the mountain, Moses did not know that the skin of his face shone because he had been talking with God. And when Aaron and all the people of Israel saw Moses, behold, the skin of his face shone and they were afraid to come near him. (Exod. 34:29, 30)

This was a dazzling religious experience that penetrated the whole personality of the prophet, such that Moses had to veil his face when speaking to the congregation, lest they be startled or nervous about this one who was so intimate with the Holy God.

These laws of God were not vague or impersonal, rather they were direct and confronting.

> And the LORD said to Moses, "Say to the people of Israel, I am the LORD your God. You shall not do as they do in the land of Egypt where you dwelt, and you shall not do as they do in the land of Canaan, to which I am bringing you. You shall not walk in their statutes. You do my ordinances and keep my statutes and walk in them. I am the LORD your God. You shall therefore keep

my statutes and my ordinances, by doing which a man shall live: I am the LORD." (Lev. 18:1–6)

Throughout the Old Testament, beginning with the people living with Moses, we trace a story of triumph and decline, success and failure in keeping the Law and staying right with God. This propensity for sin and this habit of straying and turning away from the true God bring on the preaching and guidance of the later prophets and psalmists.

It was evident to Joshua, the immediate successor to Moses, that the Lord God had great expectations for Israel, just as He expressed great wrath when the Chosen People wandered after other gods and yielded to wrong practices and shabby behavior.

When Joshua is about to enter the Promised Land (denied Moses and the people because they created a golden calf that they worshipped in the wilderness), this same Creator God deals directly with the new spiritual/political leader:

As I was with Moses, so I will be with you. I will not fail you or forsake you. Be strong and of good courage; for you shall cause this people to inherit the land which I swore to their fathers to give them. (Josh. 1:5–6)

Joshua is to lead the Israelites into a tremendous country and be the founder of this great new nation. But God knows how much these special, chosen people backslide and wander after other gods and beguiling practices of neighboring, pagan nations. How swiftly they forget, how frequently they are out of touch with the one true and living God. So a direct, personal warning appears:

Only be strong and very courageous, being careful to do according to all the law which Moses my servant commanded you; turn not from it to the right hand or to the left, that you may have good success wherever you go. This book of the law [the tablets have been codified and written] shall not depart out of your mouth, but you shall meditate on it day and night, that you may be careful to do according to all that is written in it; for then you shall make your way prosperous, and then you shall have good success. (Josh. 1:7–9)

That long quote was to become the essence of the Hebrew religion. The Law was the cornerstone of faith and practice and would become the centerpiece of the later temple sacrificial system. It has been said that by Jesus' time, the ordinances, rules, and observances exceeded 1,800 in number for the devout Jew.

The Law was mighty, practical, and personal. It was an inspiration for true believers. The nineteenth Psalm ascribed to David begins by saying,

> The heavens are telling the glory of God;
>   and the firmament proclaims his handiwork. . . .
> The law of the LORD is perfect,
>   reviving the soul;
> the testimony of the LORD is sure,
>   making wise the simple;
> the precepts of the Lord are right,
>   rejoicing the heart;
> the commandment of the LORD is pure,
>   enlightening the eyes;
> the fear of the LORD is clean,
>   enduring for ever;
> the ordinances of the LORD are true,
>   and righteous altogether.
>
>   (Ps. 19:1, 7–9)

The centrality of the Law was the past, present, and future of Israel. In its finest moments justice reigned, the poor, deprived, and orphaned were sheltered, and the na-

tion flourished in some shining centuries. The Law of the
Lord was perfect, reviving the soul. But bleak, uneasy
moments turned into decades of neglect so that an Isaiah
would shout to the Holy Israel, the Lord has spoken,

> Sons have I reared and brought up,
>   but they have rebelled against me.
> The ox knows its owner,
>   and the ass its master's crib;
> but Israel does not know,
>   my people does not understand. . . .
> They have forsaken the LORD,
>   they have despised the Holy One of Israel,
>   they are utterly estranged.
>
>   (Isa. 1:2–4)

Sin has always been translated as separation from God
and disharmony with Creation. Isaiah would pioneer new
understandings of the Law and zealous corrections of
form and practice that had been substituted for the true
observance of the ways of God. He was the one to put
down the appointed feasts and solemn assemblies, the celebration of new moons and calendar sabbaths. Ritual was
regnant; but the true religion, to "defend the fatherless
and plead for the widow" (Isa. 1:17), was desperately
lacking in Israel's priorities.

Isaiah taught the great classical themes of the Holy
Land—"come now, let us reason together, says the Lord:
though your sins are like scarlet, they shall be white as
snow, though they are red like crimson, they shall become
like wool." (Isa. 1:18)

Isaiah felt and cherished the intellectual processes, the
reasoning powers that were God-given for his people to
understand their follies and return from their sin-separa-
tion. God speaks to us through other people. He also,
argued Luther, speaks to us during our library hours and

our rational deductions. He is not separate from any level
of his Creation. And here Isaiah brought another truth to
the reality of religious experience. God is not only the one
who works through heart, head, and soul, but is drawing
other nations and peoples to himself—maybe through Israel, of all things. "It shall come to pass in the latter days,
that mountain of the LORD shall be established as the
highest of the mountains and shall be raised above the
hills; and all the nations shall flow to it." (Isa. 2:12)

Isaiah was not the first among Israel to catch this vision
of the universality of the Omnipotent God—but he was
the first to see the splendor of such a moment and gather
the yearning of people—non-Jews—to the love and justice
of God. So he wrote:

> Many peoples shall come and say: "Come, let us go up to
> the mountain of the LORD, to the house of Jacob; that
> he may teach us his ways and that we may walk in his
> paths." (Isa. 2:3)
> Then for Isaiah, as for Moses, Joshua and all the proph-
> ets and saints and seers of Israel, the might and eternity
> of the Law is proclaimed, "For out of Zion shall go forth
> the law, and the word of the Lord from Jerusalem."
> (Isa. 2:3ff.)

The result of all this? Some new conference on Mount
Sinai? A new wing to the temple of Solomon in Jerusalem? Another feast day, perhaps? Wrong. The result is
nothing less than the abolition of war, the reduction of ar-
maments, and the outbreak of global peace. Law and cov-
enant and special relationship, for Israel was to be God's
serving people, the announcers, the messengers to all
mankind. Alas, the high hopes and the most generous
aspirations of the prophets could not correct the nation of
Israel, for they were under the Law—and only the appearance of God's Son made it possible for a whole new arrangement to take place.

Paul the Apostle spotted this difficulty so clearly, for he had been a practicing Jew so zealously. And when he found the liberation of the Gospel to be deliverance from sin and death, he was able to interpret for millions of others the reality of the Resurrection of Christ instead of the rules of the old dispensation.

In Romans he would argue that

> if you call yourself a Jew and rely upon the law and boast of your relationship to God and know his will and approve what is excellent because you are instructed in the law, and if you are sure that you are a guide to the blind, a light to those who are in darkness, a corrector of the foolish, a teacher of children, having in the law the embodiment of knowledge and truth—you then who teach others, will you not teach yourself? While you preach against stealing, do you steal? . . . You who boast in the law, do you dishonor God by breaking the law? (Rom. 2:17–21, 23)

Paul had been there. He had tried professionally and personally to claim the revival of the human spirit through the majesty of the Law. The harder he pressed, the greater the failure, the larger the despair. Paul was really saying that the Law's power to convict did not give it the Christ's power to save. There must be something more personal than rules, more persuasive than ordinances and religious regulations pointing to our guilt and sin. What appeared had to be loving, personal, and of God.

The overflowing love of Jesus Christ brought men and women to the levels of ecstasy of the Spirit. The release from the burden and obligation of the Law yielded not only freedom in Christ's forgiveness but expressions of joy and celebration never before recorded in religion.

The transition from Law to love was seen dramatically in the ministry of Jonathan Edwards, the New England preacher, who ignited the Great Awakening from his parish pulpit in Northampton, Massachusetts. This famous Calvinist sharpened a theological tradition that would sweep through the colonies, embrace colleges and universities with its evangelical fervor, vault the Atlantic, and find response from Wesley and Whitfield as well.

Best known for his flaming sermon *Sinners in the Hands of An Angry God,* the preacher compelled thousands to seek the shelter of the penitent's pew. While his public message seems so searing and uncompromising, Edwards expressed the fullness of the Gospel in many vivid ways aside from the targeting of sinners for eternal damnation. He felt the wide sweep of God's love in everything—indeed, the whole point of his great revival sermon was that God was giving man another chance, still another opportunity to find the peace and forgiveness of Christ.

His bridge building between the Old Testament and the New took place in the daily events that shook the Northampton parish in the year 1734. The community experienced the sudden deaths of two young people. Edwards preached a series of sermons on Paul's great love letter, the First Epistle to the Corinthians, chapter 13. He hardly had finished when the community general store burned to the ground. Its proprietor, Deacon Ebenezer Hunt, was nearly wiped out—yet was lifted up by a massive cash purse collected from the citizens of Northampton.

Elisabeth D. Dodds, in her remarkable book, *Marriage to a Difficult Man,* writes that through Edwards' eloquent and forceful preaching two ne'er-do-wells had been converted:

The young people in the town, accustomed to meet for parties after church on Sunday evenings, began holding prayer groups instead. By December of 1734 when a young woman who had been a famous flirt said that God had "given her a new heart," Edwards reported that Religion was the one topic of conversation—scarcely a single person in the whole town was left unconcerned about the great things of the eternal world.

Edwards would trace his own born-again experience to student days at Yale. When he was just seventeen, the words of the New Testament seemed to have a singular grip on his soul: "[A]s I read the words, there came into my soul . . . a sense of glory of the Divine Being." Later his hikes and solitary walks revealed something else besides the stir of Scripture. In his *Memoirs* he writes,

> The sense I had of divine things, would often of a sudden kindle up, as it were, a sweet burning in my heart; and ardor of soul. . . . I walked abroad alone, in a solitary place in my father's pasture, for contemplation. And as I was walking there and looking up on the sky and clouds, there came into my mind so sweet a sense of the glorious majesty and grace of God, that I know not how to express. . . . God's excellency, his wisdom, his purity, and love, seemed to appear in everything: in the sun, moon, and all nature.

This evangelical tide would not only bring sinners forward but send the arts upward, for personalities such as Wordsworth would confess their dependence upon the Spirit. "I look abroad upon Nature," wrote the British poet, "I think of the best part of our species, I lean upon my friends and I meditate upon the Scriptures, especially the Gospel of St. John; and my creed rises up of itself, with the ease of exhalation yet a fabric of adamant." So fifty years later, touched by the energy and persuasion of the evangelical tide, Wordsworth penned his *Ode: In-*

timations of Immortality Recollections of Early Child-hood:

> There was a time when meadow, grove, and stream,
> The earth, and every common sight,
>> To me did seem
>> Appareled in celestial light,
> The glory and the freshness of a dream.
> O joy! that in our embers
> Is something that doth live,
> That nature yet remembers
> What was so fugitive!

The new birth of Christ in the lives of his followers would find individual expression, whether it be that of poet, preacher, or philosopher.

Jews were the first people to encounter a born-again experience. The classic New Testament setting is the encounter between Jesus and Nicodemus. A member of the Pharisee religious party, Nicodemus was a powerful civic figure, being a member of the Sanhedrin, which governed the ecclesiastical affairs of Jerusalem during Roman occupation.

Nicodemus is not only a member of the leading religious establishment but a person of keen perception and personal piety. He has followed the career of this itinerant preacher and healer from Nazareth. He is impressed by the profound teaching of the man from Galilee, but he must be careful. Jesus is not orthodox and is regarded by some as a revolutionary figure. Crowds chase him and the throng speaks about miracles. Hence Nicodemus visits Jesus at night and confesses that "you, [Rabbi], are a teacher come from God; for no one can do these signs that you do, unless God is with him."

Jesus' reply is direct and short—"Truly, truly, I say to

you, unless one is born anew, he cannot see the kingdom of God." (John 3:2, 3) This exchange reported by the gospel writer John is loaded with essential truths about the Christian life. But first a matter of translation.

BORN AGAIN

The King James Version reads "unless one is born again." The Revised Standard Version, leaning toward a more precise translation of the Greek, says "born anew." The literal Greek is "unless one is born from above"—all versions pointing to power of the Holy Spirit to lead a person in true understanding of the Christ and His being sent by God.

Nicodemus gets confused and puzzled by this necessity of rebirth. He immediately visualizes a physical birth, preceded by pregnancy and the confounding scene of a person re-entering his mother's womb. More than this, how can a person do this feat when he is old, says Nicodemus. Better yet, doing it as a teen-ager would have been just as physiologically and biologically preposterous!

Jesus keeps turning Nicodemus to the reality of the Kingdom of God, the reality of which he is announcing and confirming through his teaching. The signs, the miracles of healing, the presence of the Spirit in his ministry—all are pointing to the coming Kingdom. The New Life, the new birth, the born-again event is not connected to the dictates of the flesh but the movement of the Holy Spirit. "Good night," blurts Nicodemus, "how can this be?" And Jesus answers, "Are you a teacher of Israel and yet you do not understand this?" (John 3:10) Nicodemus was a member of the Sanhedrin and trained by the Pharisees. Many believe that Jesus' reference was to the prophetic teaching of Ezekiel known and read by Nicodemus and Jesus.

Most scholars point to the thirty-sixth chapter of Ezekiel where the Old Testament personality says that the Israelites will return from their desolation and once again inhabit a holy land that is destined for God's own people. But in their recovery of honor and the resurgence of their nationhood, conditions can no longer be the same as before—indecent, corrupt, and arrogant.

The prophet is dramatic and specific:

> I am the LORD. . . . I will take you from the nations, and gather you from all the countries and bring you into your own land. I will sprinkle clean water upon you, and you shall be clean from all your uncleannesses, and from all your idols I will cleanse you. A new heart I will give you and a new spirit I will put within you; and I will take out of your flesh the heart of stone and give you a heart of flesh. And I will put my spirit within you and cause you to walk in my statues and be careful to observe my ordinances. (Ezek. 36:23–27)

Jesus expected Nicodemus to have all this in mind. The Jewish leader certainly knew it but was not ready for the new context that Christ expressed. It is clear that this was also a practical effect of the ministry of John the Baptist—preaching a message of repentance, using the symbolic washing in the Jordan River to represent the cleansing power of God and to be the forerunner, the advance man for the coming of the Messiah.

The born-again experience first reported between Jesus and Nicodemus did not have on the surface any of the dynamics that we now associate with the term. Here was a determined search for the love and grace of God by one who had been a lifelong seeker of truth. The Mosaic law was in force and it was failing, for even the most devout were hungry for a more vital, igniting religious experience. Nicodemus did not make a public confession of faith. Nor did he admit to any major wrongdoing or disaster in his private life. But he was drawn to God through the appearance of His Son. This is the impulse of any born-again encounter.

Regarding the Pharisees, Earl Palmer writes in *The Intimate Gospel:*

> They have a very great influence with the people at large, due to their knowledge of both the law and the traditions, and also because of their admirable ethical goals. Many Pharisees fast twice a week and give money thus saved to the poor. They are intellectual; they are socially concerned moderates.

Jesus had informed Nicodemus that no one could understand that He was from God unless the Holy Spirit had given such insight and direction. But the whole purpose of that dialogue, in Jesus' eyes, was to give believing people entrance into the Kingdom of God now. The right questions, the deeper inquiry—all were fresh signs of the Kingdom's force and presence—one does not wait for death to enjoy its revealing and the fruits of that revolution.

As we trace the born-again flickering in the life of Nicodemus, we quickly see that it was not the start of one grand, happy, successful adventure, reaping bushels of happiness and boundless joy. Immediately the Jewish leader is thrust into conflict and danger. He chooses to stand by Jesus publicly and is accused himself of being a Galilean by members of that supreme council. Following the crucifixion of Jesus, Nicodemus is among those who bring spices to anoint the body. Here he is further suspect, not only to the Jews but now to the Romans who

have been keeping a sharp eye on the radical under-
ground that they were determined to control.

Nicodemus was in conflict/stress with all that was familiar and dear—his family, his temple orthodoxy and
worship patterns, his professional colleagues, and his
Roman establishment peers. But he was on the way to a
higher truth.

Again Palmer notes the Nicodemus type:

> These people are serious about knowing the will of God,
> and they really care about the truth, but they have be-
> come proud and self-righteous like anyone who develops
> a degree of expertise in such a quest. The result is that
> they are hypocritical and contemptuous toward ordinary
> people.

The born-again experience is more the spark than the
certainty of religious serenity and fulfillment. It is the ig-
nition point, the flash, the detonation moment—it cannot
be complete or final, for the Christian life is a pilgrimage and it seeks a city whose builder and maker is God.
It rests in no terminal, for it is starting out on a backpack-
ing trail.

In *The Art of Becoming a Whole Person*, Cecil Osborne
tells about a clergy counseling client who was struggling
with his own faith development as he was leading others:

> I have been preaching a very simplistic gospel, assuring
> people that when they placed all their burdens at the foot
> of the cross, they would be totally new creatures in
> Christ, with all anxieties banished and most of their prob-
> lems solved. That's a bunch of rubbish! I now realize that
> one act of repentance and a single commitment does not
> necessarily rid one of the accumulated emotional and
> spiritual debris of a lifetime. . . . I see now that after
> three years with Jesus, Simon Peter was still a mixed-up
> person. Most of the rest of the Twelve were, too. Even

living and working with him and seeing him as the Son of God did not rid them instantly or magically of their emotional hang-ups.

Martin Luther put it another way:

Life is not being religious but becoming religious, not being healthy but getting well, not being anything but becoming, not resting but working. We have not arrived, but shall do so; not yet is it finished, but it is in motion; the end is not yet, but we are on the way; not everything is bright and shining, but it is being polished.

The born-again terminology appears several times in the First Letter of Peter and brings with it an enlarged vision of the spiritual opportunities awaiting Christian believers. The letter was written as an epistle of encouragement. The author is believed to be St. Peter. The import and emphasis are clear: "By his great mercy we have been born anew to a living hope through the resurrection of Jesus Christ from the dead, and to an inheritance which is imperishable, undefiled, and unfading, kept in heaven for you. . . ." (1 Pet. 1:3–4)

The new being in Christ, the born-anew experience, and the revival of the spirit were seen as the introduction not only to the joys and satisfactions of the Kingdom of God (an inheritance that is "imperishable, unfading") but the entrance into an exhilarating fellowship that made life bearable.

Many of the first converts, including these addressed by Peter, were sensing the loss and disarray from the historic roots of Judaism and the anchor site of Jerusalem. They were displaced throughout Asia and the cities encircling the Mediterranean. Their feeling of being religious refugees was keen and sharp.

So if one is truly found in the revival of the soul by

being born anew, what were the practical results of such a commitment?

The epistle writer senses this puzzlement and even apprehension of former Jews who must have shared a homesickness for the security of Israel and the protection of a Promised Land. Jesus is the cornerstone of their faith; he is the one pointed to by the prophets. His sacrifice on the Cross eradicates and abolishes all the other sacrifices of men in an old and worn system. He is the true high priest because he offers spiritual sacrifices that do not depend on the slaughtering of animals or the keeping of special seasons. But more—his Kingdom is breaking forth, not the turf of Palestine but actually the Kingdom of God Himself!

Briefly the message was that by the renewing of the Holy Spirit in your lives, not only are you born again into a lasting, living fellowship but you have citizenship that far exceeds all the excitement and grandeur of Israel and Judah. Gathering some of the lofty phrases of the New Testament, indeed of human literature itself, the author says that now, "You are a chosen race, a royal priesthood, a holy nation, God's own people, that you may declare the wonderful deeds of him who called you out of darkness into his marvelous light." (1 Pet. 2:9–10) And there rests a new aspect of the born-again agenda—to point, lead, direct, and encourage others in their love of God . . . to recognize that we are in the presence of God.

Jesus said we cannot *see* the Kingdom of God unless we are born anew. There is evidence in almost every life that we have strayed from a true sense of wonder and a deep feeling of thanksgiving to God for all that we are and all that we have received. Our loss of vision is the absence of the true light, and our lack of sight is the unwillingness to look beyond the present, obvious, and the immediate.

Nothing is more real than God's presence and God's unfolding Kingdom, said the Savior. I do not come to reveal wonders, perform the miraculous, or dazzle the doubters —I come to point to the ultimate, lasting reality—belonging to the God who has made you for His lasting Kingdom, a community founded on love and expressed through justice and forgiveness.

Jesus burst upon the sedate, tired landscape of Palestine with the urgency and confidence of a prophet—only more. To the dumbfounded audience at Nazareth he said (reading the Sabbath lesson for that hour):

> The spirit of the Lord is upon me because he has
>   anointed me;
> he has sent me to announce good news to the poor,
> to proclaim release for prisoners and recovery of
>   sight to the blind
> to let the broken victims go free,
> to proclaim the year of the Lord's favor.
>   (Luke 4:18–19 NEB)

The congregation was not stunned because Jesus read so clearly but because he said that this prophecy was now fulfilled in their hearing. The announcement of the Kingdom was his to make, but only those spiritually prepared, like Nicodemus, perhaps, could "see it."

Jesus added another slant to this spiritual awakening. Unless one is born of water and the Spirit, he cannot *enter* the Kingdom of God, heard Nicodemus.

Unless a person seeks to drastically remodel his or her life, to challenge the false values of a secular society, to face down the priority system of a commercial, racist world, to step away from the idolatry of our modern scene, unless one is prepared to be baptized and honestly link your life with His, we cannot enter the Kingdom of God. Jesus said to his disciples, "let the children come to me, and do not hinder them; for of such belongs the kingdom of heaven." (Matt. 19:14) To be close to birth, to be nearer to the dependency and frailty and wonder of infancy, to put our whole trust and commitment to God, only then do we start to find the true cathedral, God's presence in our soul, to worship and really be at home with him and others and ourselves.

2

From Conversion
to Community

Conversion draws us into a new relationship—the Christian community helps us to validate, authenticate, and elaborate on our born-again, born from above event. But will Christians really accept a Colson, a Cleaver? The threat of celebrity conversions.

SOME INITIAL CONCLUSIONS ABOUT CONVERSION

The first thing we discover about the born-again experience in the New Testament is that it is *rational,* linking the individual with God through Christ—and with other believers. When Jesus announced the emergence of the Kingdom of God, he was inviting followers into a divine/human companionship. *The solitary Christian experience does not exist in the New Testament*—and one can question whether such an individual scene is at all possible for any Christian in any time. (I realize that there are solitary, enforced moments for Christian persons—a confining illness, a prison experience suffered by Christian people ever since Paul, or some painful personal exile as lived by Alexander Solzhenitsyn in Kazakhstan. These are individual heroic settings—but not the norm or standard for the Christian fellowship of believers who share in the breaking of bread and the preaching of the word.)

This relational experience is constantly evident in the life of St. Peter and in the conversion of St. Paul. When Peter is out of touch with his fellow disciples—and his Master, he ends up falling asleep and failing to warn Jesus of his approaching arrest. When Jesus is taken for questioning, Peter, alone, denies at least three times that he has anything to do with the Son of God. So we are hardly surprised at the post-Easter experience—really counseling—between the Risen Christ and Peter where Jesus asks him to feed his lambs, tend his sheep, feed his sheep, with the clinching statement, "When you turn again, Peter, and find your faith strong, strengthen your brothers."

The Christian life was an incendiary fellowship. Spiritual sparks ignited when believers were sharing the deepest moments of their earthly life, recounting the joys and marvels that Jesus had made real and personal.

This relational key sent Peter into a stunning leadership role—when he was with the others and speaking for the Christian cause now so primary and central to his whole existence. From the first chapter on, the book of Acts sets a torrid pace with Peter standing among the disciples and calling for the election of a replacement of Judas. This completed with the choosing of Matthias, Peter next preaches on the day of Pentecost, sweeping thousands into the broadening Christian community, and stirring the city of Jerusalem to fresh amazement at the persuasion of such an unscholarly, unlettered "blue-collar" preacher. Event after event dramatizes the unique living fellowship that Peter had with the other disciples and what Peter especially communicated to new converts. At last the signs of the Kingdom are convincing—and invincible, for we then read in Acts, chapter 4:

> Now the company of those who believed were of one heart and soul, and no one said that any of the things which he possessed was his own, but they had everything in common. And with great power the apostles gave their testimony to the resurrection of the Lord Jesus, and great grace was upon them all. There was not a needy person among them. . . . (Acts 4:32–34)

If we are to have a growing, enduring life with Christ, it will be found in the companionship of his people. And the Christian life is the one experience that links hopefulness with helpfulness. Most of us share the pursuit of this religious commitment with others from our own community. Our congregation may be in our neighborhood or across town. But generally it is operative within driving distance of our homes. But there are times when we share faith far across the boundaries of town and state. Let me explain one such happening.

One year a woman telephoned from the airport. She was changing planes, returning to another state following a short vacation on the West Coast. She was aware of our ministry in Albuquerque through the comments of a mutual friend. Did we have time for her to visit and discuss a personal problem that was about to destroy her marriage?

When she arrived a few moments later (our church is just ten minutes from the airport), I wondered if there was anything that could be of benefit in such a hurried, between-flights visit. Yet her urgency was so great and her need so pressing that she plunged directly to the heart of her problem—and it was a matter of the heart.

Her marriage had lasted fourteen years and she doubted if it would continue another twelve months. While she loved and enjoyed her three children, her affection and regard for her husband had vanished. He was boring, insensitive, and distant . . . totally wrapped up in his work and removed from the emotional needs of her life or that of their children. Alas, in the midst of this despair, she had confided in a family friend and discovered his love for her and she for him. This clandestine, adulterous relationship had offered new levels of excitement and adventure for her. The hide and seek of their affair, the romantic indulgence, and the sexual expectation was overwhelming. She believed in Christian marriage, the sanctity of the home, the integrity of marital vows; but they were under severe test, especially with the aggravating distance and aloofness of her spouse. She wanted permission to pursue this liaison, but something within was holding her back, calling her to take another look at this unfolding tragedy.

Our meeting was not long, but the developing correspondence revealed several vital truths—that men and women frequently face low times in their marriage and that selfishness rates high above service in a society that rates pleasure first and responsibility a cheap second. Her life and her marriage, if it was to survive, required more support and strength than she had within her personality. It could only prevail with the love and strength of God and the honesty that she at last poured out in prayer.

Upon return to her home city, this airport visitor began to seek the fellowship of her church, the entry into long conversations with God and the opportunity to give service to others. But most important, the real clue to her new life in the Spirit was the courage to inquire, within a long period of prayer and daily quiet hours, if it really was God's will that she sever this marriage and disrupt her children's young life. Not only was she given spiritual direction from God but also surprising, fresh insights on how to help her husband deal with his role in a creative partnership.

In one of his books, Robert Raines says simply, "It takes time to become a Christian." This traveling friend from another city discovered that she had hardly taken time to let the Christian life blossom. The watering and cultivation and caring had yet to happen. Raines goes on to say that "if conversion is to be permanent, decision must lead into growth and be sustained by discipline." He suggests that the community of faith is always represented in six activities or disciplines. The more we share and seek the fulfillment of these time investments, the more powerful and sustaining becomes our belief in Christ.

In *New Life in the Church* Raines lists corporate worship, daily prayer, bible reading, giving, service, and witness as six necessary disciplines. It's interesting to note that the last three can not happen without the first three. If our giving is meager, our service grudging, and our witness nonexistent, then the first three values never get into our personalities.

Rev. Donald Shelby once recounted the following illustration to his congregation:

> A certain doctor, who was Christ's follower, gave time to a charity clinic. One day an elderly gentleman was ushered into this physician's private office downtown. "Remember me, Doctor?" asked the man. "You've treated me over at the clinic. I've gotten a little ahead so I can afford to come to a private office." "But what made you come to me?" the Doctor wanted to know. "I wasn't the only physician on the clinic staff." "I know," the old man said quietly, "but you were the only one who helped me with my coat."

The living fellowship keeps us close to the fires of God, and in warming ourselves, we are able to bring care and warmth to others.

The early born-again people were in community, they were linked by a shared treasure in the life and death and Resurrection of Jesus. The fire of their fellowship glowed, attracting others. The power of their message was contagious and convicting, so that people would say, What shall we do?

And today the same question arrives—what shall we

do? The resurgence of the religious revival is everywhere affecting thousands upon thousands. While we dare not judge another person's confession of faith as being authentic or false, of being a fad or a faithful response, we can say that it will wither and die unless it be lived out in a Christian community. The relational aspect of the Christian church causes one's spiritual adventure to gain new depth and height, drawing in a divine way the support, loving criticism, and encouragement of others.

When we review the turmoil and upheaval that accompanied the conversion of St. Paul on the road to Damascus—when he would be given even a new name, Paul in place of Saul—when we see the strenuous, daring forces at work, this tells us of the courage and determination of Christians to be faithful to Jesus in giving Saul a chance to articulate his change of heart and his rebirth as a Christian follower. This Pharisee, this Christian headhunter would enter a major personal transformation. But first his massive evil enterprise must be smashed. Saul, you remember, was struck blind by the light flashing from heaven; he cannot rise but does hear the voice of Jesus asking him to cease this persecution of His followers. Saul is brought, stumbling and sightless, to Damascus where he begins praying but does not eat or drink for three days.

Ananias, a local Christian, is led by the Spirit to announce Paul's healing and return to sight all in the name of the Risen Christ. His vision returns and he is immediately baptized—born again by the water and the word through the power of the Spirit. But it is not a private moment of piety, a solitary soul being won to God, for we then read, "For several days he was with the disciples at Damascus. And in the synagogues immediately he proclaimed Jesus, saying, 'He is the Son of God.'" (Acts

22:9–10) Conversion draws us into a new relationship, and the Christian community helps us to validate, authenticate, and elaborate on our born-again, born from above event. In every true account from Scripture, it is just the beginning of a great adventure in faith.

3

Celebrity Conversions—
Help or Hindrance
for the Church?

In the last half dozen years a celebrity system has developed within the Christian family. Does publicity advance or hinder the Christian community?

Not only is the born-again moment the beginning of new relational values, it reaches to unfold a revolutionary aspect that we may not be prepared to grasp or affirm. But it is there from the beginning, and when alive and surging, very present today. And the revolutionary changes that matter are the deep alterations of the heart. Before his assassination, the Black Muslim leader, Malcolm X, wrote in his papers:

> I believe that it would be impossible to find anywhere in America a black man who has lived further down in the mud of human society than I have . . . or a black man who has suffered more anguish during his life than I have. But it is only after the deepest darkness that the greatest light can come; it is only after extreme grief that the greatest joy can come.

These were prophetic words spoken by Malcolm X concerning himself, but they surely apply to Eldridge Cleaver. The former Black Panther was a distant and constant admirer of Malcolm X. Cleaver had gotten so deeply into the Muslim prison group in California prisons that everyone assumed he would be the West Coast leader of the militant religious sect, which split between Muhammad Elijah and Malcolm X.

Prior to his deep attachment to the Muslim cause,

Cleaver had been a teen-age criminal in East Los Angeles, emerging as a hustling gangster (one of the few ever admitted to the Mexican Mafia ring on the West Coast) and then a professional rapist and drug dealer. Cleaver's rage toward America and its injustices toward blacks found a welcome formula in the Black Panther–Black Muslim theology that finally emerged. Although slated for great things in the mosque of the California Muslims, Cleaver opted for national leadership with the Panther Party out of Oakland.

His days and nights were filled with journeys through the valley of the shadow of death. Some people believed that Eldridge was the enforcer for the Panthers. Others knew him as an eloquent speaker who challenged the white racist police-state attitudes of America in the sixties. Many in the civil rights movement applauded his nerve while hesitant over his gun-brandishing tactics. The peace movement and the anti-Vietnam War coalitions cheered him on as he rose in rhetoric against the war in Southeast Asia. Indeed, some of the most vociferous members of the growing Panther Party were returned veterans—with armament training and battlefield bravado. It was a daring, dangerous, deadly time.

When Cleaver and others were drawn into an Oakland shoot-out with local police, the Panther minister of education was arrested and accused of killing a police officer. Pleading his innocence and fearful of a rigged trial, Cleaver escaped to Algeria and became a communist celebrity, joining speech making and writing all over the other world.

However, the six years of observation, travel, and conversation in the Marxist countries with their Stalin legacy proved to be a shattering experience for Cleaver. He was smart enough and honest enough to admit it was one thing to recognize the distortions of freedom in America—and quite another to witness the destruction of freedom under the Communists.

From the beginning of his spiritual odyssey, Cleaver told his friends that the conversion to Christ was not a sudden, overnight happening. The birth of his son and the joy of that new young life began to undercut and erode the rigid, materialistic doctrines of Marxism. The followers of Marx, Lenin, and Stalin had no place for creative joy, no recognition of the emerging spirit and soul of a baby. Cleaver marked well the ideological contrast. The death of his father was another jar for Eldridge—plus the fact that he could not join the clan—of which he was the recognized head—because of his exile and fugitive status overseas.

All his heroes had failed. All his gods were dead: Marx, Stalin, and Castro had no appeal, no enduring orders, no ultimate values that mattered or were enforceable. And within his own spirit, he felt the decay and rot and sickness unto death that only the truth of the Gospel, the winning words of Christ could restore and renew.

Today Cleaver is one of the surprising, even sensational voices in the Christian community. His personal change—to use an overworked term—is truly revolutionary. For like his hero, Malcolm X, he had sunk low and was lost. Now he is a whole new person in Christ. A sign that revolutions not only affect nations and kingdoms and empires, but ever so thrillingly, the citadel of the soul.

CRISES FOR THE CHURCH: CELEBRITY CONVERSIONS

In the last half dozen years a celebrity system has developed within the Christian family. Men and women have gained fame through their sensational born-again stories and now exert enormous influence in the minds of the faithful. Most powerful and visible is the President of the United States who has spoken freely and frequently about his own conversion moment. Jimmy Carter is the most visible Christian layman in public office since Eisenhower and the most theologically oriented since Woodrow Wilson. It's intriguing to note that all of these mentioned had a Calvinistic worldview and a driving desire to bring the benefits of their religion to the opportunities of their elected office.

When Jimmy Carter campaigned for the nomination and then went on to win the general election, many secular writers expressed alarm and apprehension about having such a spiritual person in the White House. Would it mean an unusual leverage for the Southern Baptists? How would Carter deal with the moral complexities of foreign affairs? One Washington correspondent phoned this writer to satisfy his anxieties over Carter's ability to control a suspected messianic streak in the new position. "I mean," he said, "what if Carter thinks it is God's will to zap the Russians for their ungodly behavior or unrighteous dealings with neighboring states. With Carter's conservative indoctrination, he may launch us into a catastrophic holy war over a new Berlin crisis or a Middle East confrontation. Can we trust a born-again Christian to be deliberate, restrained, and patient with all the moral ambiguities that go with the job in the Oval Office of the White House?"

I responded that the answer would only come in the months and years ahead, yet any study of the New Testament and any sensitivity to the wider Baptist community would reveal how off-base were his near hysterical observations of the new President.

In many respects Christians with a high visibility in the
Congress have a beautiful opportunity to reflect the practical aspects that belong to the spiritual commitment of
their lives. When we consider the public stance of Sen.
Mark Hatfield on so many difficult and puzzling controversies, it is refreshing to have insights and point of view
shared with the larger public. His deep and persistent
questioning of the war in Vietnam, his sensitive advocacy
of Palestinian rights in Israel, his challenge of racist and
sexist policies in government have come from the caring
mind and heart of a born-again Christian. People like
Mark Hatfield, Harold Hughes, Strom Thurmond, and
Charles Percy have given Christians in Congress a style of
companionship even when they must differ and disagree
on particular items of debate. The Senate Prayer Group,
which I have attended, was a unique and inspiring exchange, prayers, and concerns by people in government
who were also in Christ.

There must be recognized, however, the inherent dan-
gers that accompany the high visibility of public office
and civic leadership. Consider the first prayer breakfast
under President Carter. It was a major winter event for
Washington. It had the social requirements of attendance
as does a St. Patrick's Day Parade for marching among
the Irish. More than a thousand were present when you
include the overflow rooms at the Mayflower. The leading
dignitaries and power persons in government were in
charge. Everyone endorsed morality, the teachings of
Jesus, and the efficacy of prayer. After all, it was a prayer
breakfast for the people serving in public office, so the
major prayer/address was given by none other than Bert
Lance.

The risks of celebrity Christians are not going to diminish but increase, for they are the requirements of living

and working with a culture feeding, following, and foster-
ing mass media. And with the grand reach that accompa-
nies a global communications system of television, with
the enormous audience and instant appeal, so also are the
danger and destructive results that accrue without our
beckoning.

When Billy Graham conducted a major crusade in the
Philippines, his host for a state dinner was no other than
President Marcos—considered by many to be the first
Spanish dictator in the Pacific. Graham went on to have a
successful series of preaching events in the Philippine Islands, but many devoted Christians were embarrassed
and injured by the linking of a gospel personality with a
cunning political leader.

The celebrity Christians right now are those persons
who either display amazing gifts of healing and prophecy
or have had an almost cosmic alteration in their personality and life style. Perhaps the most notorious is Eldridge
Cleaver. His life had been so shocking and his rhetoric so
cutting that no one a decade ago could have imagined
such colossal religious reorientation in our day. Cleaver
was really the enemy, not only to the principles of Christianity but to the major tenets of Western civilization and
the free world. When his publisher invited me to work
with him in an editorial capacity, to assist in the produc-
tion and writing of his new book, *Soul on Fire,* I was
sharply apprehensive. Could such a dangerous personality
be trusted? Was his conversion authentic or just his way
of getting a free trip back to America and sympathy for
his postponed trial in Oakland?

The credibility gap between Cleaver and the wider
Christian community was serious. He stood to capitalize
handsomely on his television guest appearances, and the
box-office demand that now sought him for major speak-

ing appearances on college tours, Christian conventions, and laity conferences. Conservative Christians had put up thousands to cover his bond expense and trial costs—trusting that God was at work in this distorted life now come to Christ.

My own experience was satisfying—to meet and work and live with a new Christian who hungered for the word of God and who was living a life of prayer and private devotion. There was no question that Eldridge was living off the celebrity status and the big fees that networks and publishers and speaking bureaus could generate. But he was also bringing a fresh dynamic to the Christian scene in America. He was bright and alert and eager—eager to share the rebirth of his soul and the Resurrection of Jesus Christ in his own existence.

Cleaver lives the three R's of conversion today—the relational, the revolutionary, and the relevant. Much of his own study/discussion growth has come under the influence of the Peninsula Church in Palo Alto, California, where Ray Stedman has had a unique and inspiring ministry. This pastor-theologian included Cleaver in his weekly Bible studies, enlarging the base and extending the vision of the Christian enterprise for the former black militant.

Cleaver in turn not only shared the dynamics of his conversion with a national audience around America, but also devoted countless hours to leading Bible study sessions with former Black Muslims who were practically religious strays in the Bay Area. The former Black Panther leader knew their angry resentments toward whites, their distrust of Christianity, and their rage toward "fortress America," which seemed to have them carefully targeted for destruction. Skilled in Marxism as well as the philosophy of the Black Muslims, Cleaver has become the bridge person to a new life and hope for many who have despaired of life and of themselves.

A celebrity such as Cleaver will also have enormous influence in the prison society in America once his own case is cleared. He knows the structure and sickness that affects so much of our penal system, and he is prepared with the direction and counsel of Christians in and out of the government to deal with the problems of crime and punishment and correction.

A personage such as Eldridge Cleaver also may give the black churches a shot in the arm, for when he appears, *men* as well as women turn out to hear his message. He does not oppose or resist integration but wants to affirm the gospel gifts of black Christians as they deal with the frontal problems of ghetto life. Eldridge knows this turf, the rejections and remorse of such a situation, and the hope that comes from the sustaining spirit of Christ. This celebrity may be shocking and notorious, and to some threatening, but so, alas, was St. Paul.

The most damaging aspects of the Christian celebrity syndrome is the manipulation and misquotation that the secular press puts upon these personalities. The hostile atmosphere of too many writers and news editors toward the integrity of a born-again person is something to behold. It may be that those caught up in the secular combat of mass media today feel that they must hack away at every affirmation, every pronouncement, every proposal that comes from a notorious convert. A second aspect may be even deeper than building one's reputation on put-down articles concerning famous evangelists or itinerant faith healers—the reporting person may wish to present a tough, outer shell, a know-it-all cynicism, unwilling to admit any personal religious convictions—or emotions supporting that faith.

LIABILITIES FOR THE BORN-AGAIN CELEBS

Recently *Sojourners* magazine noted with dismay that Eldridge Cleaver had designed some new clothes for men's fashion wear, featuring a rather prominent cod piece that highlighted the location of the male sex organ. During that same period, *Christianity Today* reported that:

> Former Black Panther, Eldridge Cleaver, was scratched from the program by a last minute action of the National Religious Broadcasters, which was distressed by Cleaver's recently announced intention to market a controversial style of men's jeans.

(Both Cleaver and *Hustler* publisher, Larry Flynt, became an unresolved problem for this Washington convention; their names did not appear on the printed program.) What was not apparent to the reading, religious public was that Cleaver had begun designing clothes during his sojourn in France as a fugitive from justice in America. Cleaver had become fascinated by the vast clothing industry as well as dollars to be made in fashion-conscious Paris. Following some initial drawings, he invited, through advertisements in the European edition of the *New York Herald Tribune,* interested parties to invest in this fashion adventure. As I recall his comments to me during 1977, many inquiries followed, and several businesses were ready to start producing this "revolutionary" line of men's wear. Whether you like cod-patch designs better than Levi's zippers is up to the taste and style of the purchaser, I suspect. What irritated *So-*

journers and others who learned of this manufacturing project was that it seemed out of keeping with the born-again spiritual priorities of Mr. Cleaver.

Cleaver's creative brilliance is not just confined to conservative theology. There are definite possibilities that he may become a nationally syndicated columnist or a television personality commenting on people in the news. His way with words, his writing style, and his fame as a global celebrity extend into a whole network of current issues and controversies. He was among the first in North America to identify Castro's African adventures as the agency of Russian military encroachment into the Horn of Africa. (Clever also reported firsthand on the "training camps" for revolutionaries who were too hot for Castro to handle. It has been Cleaver's contention that Ché Gueverra was too radical and threatening to Fidel Castro and was given front-line assignments in Africa—and South America—in order to dispose of him as a rival. Correct interpretation or not—it worked.)

The life style of Eldridge Cleaver may disturb some Christians. He likes to operate on the high level of management—first-class hotels, a busy and aggressive staff to handle his office, correspondence, bookings, and reservations. He maintains a professional-level library of clippings and notes on everything—especially the gossip about old Black Panthers—which he observes can now be identified as Black Hamsters.

In truth, Cleaver has never *not* been a celebrity. His criminal activities from high school on gave him a certain renown in California correctional facilities. Anyone who carries a .38 for ten years and admits to being a professional rapist is going to have a certain amount of notoriety. As an advanced teacher in the Black Muslim movement and one-time heir to leadership in the California franchise, he was followed and respected in that whole arena, in and out of prison.

His Marxist fascination and communist affiliations finally linked him up with the Black Panthers, and in less than two years, he was in the inner circle of national leadership. *Soul on Ice* gave him an identification as a savvy revolutionary all over the world and brought him a massive flow of correspondence and dollars and a lot of copy and play with the news editors.

Now it's all different. As a born-again Christian, Cleaver gets a big yawn from the Eastern press. Eldridge is no longer hot copy for the Sunday *Times*. He hasn't frightened the Zionists for at least seven years with his Algerian-based oratory.

And on the fashionable, trendy topics of today's journalists, such as advocacy of homosexual rights, Cleaver is not providing supportive headlines. He doesn't say, "Right On, Brother," or "Off the Pig" anymore. Forget the clenched fist salute, let Andrew Young do that—Eldridge has been there and back.

I don't believe that he owns a black leather jacket and the single earring is missing. When you see him at the airport today, goodness, he's wearing a suit with a vest and carrying a briefcase, and he's smiling!

The *Times* wants to cover terrorism—not converted urban guerrillas. And *Newsweek* wants threatening speeches and four-letter words and pools of blood, and CBS would rather film a Marin County shoot-out or sixty minutes with someone who is not a lay preacher expounding on the virtues and joys of the Christian life. Well, people, they all will have to be satisfied with Idi Amin, for Eldridge Cleaver is a Soul on Fire.

Pondering some of the irritations and irreverences of

the new Eldridge Cleaver and noting some of the unique contributions he can make to the Christian advance as the people of God move to the twenty-first century, I remembered what Page Smith said about Thomas Jefferson, another North American celebrity who lived in France at a much earlier period and had the capacity to confound friends and critics simultaneously:

> Despite periodic grumblings among his colleagues and open admonishments from the bolder, they kept choosing him for important and responsible offices, which suggest a remarkable gift for drawing people to him.

> Indeed, we must assume that he had charm or charisma, a quality of tact and a delicacy of feeling that made his friends willing to overlook rather substantial deficiencies. Charisma is often characterized by passions under somewhat precarious control—a burning inner intensity is an essential element in this strange and ultimately inexplicable power that certain people exercise over others. Great capacity for suffering has a strong power of attraction.

Another aspect that permeates media today is a firm resistance to the truths of the Gospel and a severe enforcing attitude to stymie or thwart the impact of what Christians are trying to say. Does a sports figure turn to Christ? His new life is greeted with mocking respect and withering sarcasm by the reporters who thought he was just fine as the old drinking, whoring gridiron star they loved to cover in last year's season. His plunge into a new life style is not only bewildering to nonbelievers but absolutely threatening. Now Joe Football Kingdom is saying that the old world is junk, that sin has lost its seductive glamour, and change is the only way out. A lot of guys and dolls in the sports desk just do not want to rearrange their lives because their favorite after-game, bar-hopping buddy is now a Jesus freak. Rather than face the reality of lives like their own, which are disappointing and unfulfilling, they will seek out another idol who can live up to the flaky life someone has just denied. Conversion does affect people negatively, creating anger, rage, and depression. And especially journalistic put-downs.

Christian celebrities soon learn that they are not only carrying their own program but the baggage of others as well. The most prominent Christian woman in North America today is Ruth Carter Stapleton, the President's sister. Whatever you think of her speaking style, the doctrine that enforces her healing skills, or the contact she has with Larry Flynt and other notorious converts, you must acknowledge that she is mentally equipped to handle the rigors of her public ministry. Intellectually, she is at home in the wide field of psychotherapy and well read in the history of psychology. Although a Southern Baptist, she would be at home in almost any mainline denomination today, for she represents a generous view of Scripture, uncluttered by any legalism or literalism that was a hallmark of evangelists a decade ago, especially those with charismatic gifts. Her health and holiness are evident in her writings. Her influence extends broadly in the whole Christian community, affecting a great variety of Catholics, as well as liberal Protestants.

Yet her ministry was nearly poisoned by a long, rambling speculative article which appeared in *Newsweek*. Identifying her as Sister Ruth (and all the connotations of earlier women evangelists, good, bad, and beautiful), the essay portrayed her as a with-it, born-again Christian who was at home in modern psych and often abroad with Larry Flynt. When not seeing the founder of *Hustler* magazine, she was supposedly on the phone everyday with her most famous convert.

Developing an "I'm O.K., Your Theology is O.K." style of describing the present theology of this Christian celebrity, *Newsweek* went on to quote her saying:

> I believe that when Jesus was in the Garden of Gethsemane, what he willingly took upon himself was the subconscious of the whole human race.

That must have been an unwelcome surprise to millions of orthodox Christians who support her work and endorse her ministry. It was as if the word "sin" was stale and the more trendy term, "subconscious," more fitting to appear in the pages of a national newsweekly.

But more,

> I believe that Jesus was just a man, but a man who was ordained by God to carry the burden of all the negative thoughts and feelings of all human beings who ever lived. And I believe that through the Holy Spirit, God can be in me just as he was in Jesus.

That little grenade detonated all over the Christian map, with Ruth getting slammer phone calls and conference leaders wondering if Mrs. Stapleton was really the speaker they ought to have as a model for the Christian witness in our time.

The clincher that rattled all the doors of the assembly hall where the members of the Christian Booksellers Association were meeting in Colorado Springs the summer of 1978 was simply, "Personally, I rely on Jesus, but who knows, maybe God was in Buddha just like he was in Jesus."

Ruth Carter Stapleton finally got a chance in a press conference reported in the *Rocky Mountain News* (July

18, 1978) to answer the twenty-one errors contained in the magazine article. She affirmed her belief in the divinity of Jesus, grandly blurred by the reporters in *Newsweek*. She also noted that she was not breathlessly in daily touch with Larry Flynt, that it was more like every two weeks. She confessed her faith in the bodily resurrection of Jesus Christ, "who died for my sins upon the Cross." She admitted that reading some of the quotes projected in the article, "was the most devastating experience in my life." (When warned by a *Newsweek* staffer that some of the material in the proposed religious essay on her would "make your hair stand on end," she asked why. The answer in reply, she said, was "This is *Newsweek* and we have to be controversial sometimes.")

This reckless, and often mindless, uproar created by news sources is going to be with us for a long time and is going to haunt religious personalities who are out front, exposed, and open to the ridicule and suspicion that such a climate so easily designs and then promotes.

One does not expect Christian leaders to be spared this excess any more than are their secular counterparts currently being whipsawed in the news media. When Alexander Solzhenitsyn gave his stinging speech to Harvard graduates of the Class of 1978, he camped on this theme and cried against it:

> The press, too, of course, enjoys the widest freedom (I shall be using the word "press" to include all the media). But what use does it make of it? . . .

> There is no true moral responsibility for distortion or disproportion. What sort of responsibility does a journalist or a newspaper have to the readership or to history . . .

Because instant and credible information is required, it becomes necessary to resort to guesswork, rumors, and suppositions to fill in the voids, and none of them will ever be refuted; they settle into the readers' memory. How many hasty, immature, superficial, and misleading judgments are expressed every day, confusing readers, and are then left hanging? The press can act the role of public opinion or miseducate it."

4

The Dangers and the Blessings of Publicized Conversions

The promotional zeal of some Christian personalities borders on pure huckstering. . . . [T]o be a Christian is to put up with, at times, a whole lot of bunk from others who want to market the gospel experience for their own gain.

Just as mass media has its own special indulgences and temptations to power, so do those within the Christian community who have access to commercial and promotional devices. The current rage of the Jesus fad is to stick some random quote from Scripture on bumper stickers, T-shirts, and articles of clothing and jewelry.

Christian bookstores can now carry a religious T-shirt for your dog, complete with Bible phrase and prominently positioned Cross. Bumper stickers, playing off the popularity of *Star Wars* now read:

> The FORCE IS WITH ME
> . . . his name is JESUS!

For those who want a more practical application of their faith, buy a child's bib that says, "Jesus Loves All Us Kids." For the religious executive, there is a package for the office called: "Faithful Desk Accessories," including a letter opener with a logo: "Rejoicing in the Lord."

However, I don't wish to be insensitive to the beginners' slopes of Christianity. Not long ago my wife and I rode up the mile-long chair lift at Purgatory Ski Area in western Colorado. The twenty-five-minute trip soared above rocks and pine trees, offering a breathtaking glimpse of the southern Rockies. By the time we reached the summit we were ten thousand feet above sea level. The air was bracing and cold. The view almost world-wide, it seemed. We trembled from excitement and exhilaration of such a moment. I observed other lifts down below tracing separate patterns up the broad, high mountains. At the very bottom was a rope tow, reserved for beginners and tugging them gently and slowly to a mild downhill run. Also, For Beginners, No Charge, said the sign. People have to start somewhere and there are easy, comfortable, and inexpensive ways for that to happen.

That is a living parable of the Praise the Lord Club. They have a winning slogan, for the praise of God belongs daily in the heart of every true Christian. It is the supportive framework of the Gospel—to give praise and thanks to God.

This media church is also a beginners' slope, reminding us that new converts and fresh novices require small doses of responsibility and expectations. This is crib-level Christianity—the entertainment of the children's story, the catchy songs and smiling faces, the use of color and sound and emotion for a worthy cause. But if it becomes the goal, the final resting place for the Christian enterprise in the last half of the twentieth century, the party is over.

St. Paul knew the tender sentiments of beginning believers. He had been there once and then grew up to stature in the faith, becoming its foremost apostle. So he could write out of firsthand experience, a remembrance of those first fragile moments of proclaiming the living Christ:

> When I came to you brethren, I did not come to you proclaiming to you the testimony of God in lofty words or wisdom. For I decided to know nothing among you ex-

cept Jesus Christ, and him crucified. And I was with you in weakness and in much fear and trembling; and my speech and my message were not in plausible words of wisdom but in demonstration of the Spirit and power, that your faith might not rest in the wisdom of men but in the power of God. (1 Cor. 2:1–5)

Paul was giving some confidential reflections to that sophisticated Christian community at Corinth. They were no dummies. They had worked through the upper range of Greek philosophy. Roman law was on their lips. Hebrew sayings were not misquoted. But they were new Christians, hesitant and provisional, and Paul spoke to that emptiness and need.

The promotional zeal of some Christian personalities borders on pure huckstering. The art form seems to be to coin as much money on the up-front aspects of the conversion event and combining it with grade C record albums, personally conducted tours of the Holy Lands, and a whole series of books dealing with a star's religious life. This becomes dishonest and boring. It offers to the public a perversion of Christianity and eventually brings dishonor to the cause of Christ. To be a Christian is to put up with a lot of bunk from other believers who want to market the gospel experience for their own gain.

But even this is present in the New Testament. There were many in Jesus' time who felt it natural and obligatory that they demonstrate constantly their religious devotion and prowess for the benefit of other people. It was a society and era that put great stock in the public example of religiosity. So Jesus urged his people to

Beware of practicing your piety before men in order to be seen by them; for then you will have no reward from your Father who is in heaven.

Thus, when you give alms, sound no trumpet before you, as the hypocrites do in the synagogues and in the streets, that they may be praised by men. Truly I say to you, they have their reward.

And when you pray, you must not be like the hypocrites; for they love to stand and pray in the synogogues and at the street corners, that they may be seen by men. Truly I say to you, they have their reward. But when you pray, go into your room and shut the door and pray your Father who is in secret; and your Father who sees in secret will reward you. (Matt. 6:1–2, 5–7)

Right now the PTL Club is the biggest show in Christendom if you count the playing hours they have on syndicated cable television. While such a program may be supportive to shut-ins and possibly helpful to new believers, its stance violates almost every one of the above directions given by Jesus to his followers. The touting of individual success stories and the incessant appeal for funds run on hour after hour. The impression is one of a highly individualized form of religion, a distinct absence of a worshipping community that has obligations and responsibilities outside the studio lights, and a nomenclature, a vocabulary, of faith that is juvenile, indeed.

So Paul continues this out-loud reminiscence when he continues to write;

But I, brethren, could not address you as spiritual men, but as men of the flesh, as babes in Christ. I fed you with milk, not solid food; for you were not ready for it; and even yet you are not ready, for you are still of the flesh. For while there is jealousy and strife among you, are you not of the flesh, and behaving like ordinary men? (1 Cor. 3:1–3)

The danger of the spiritual-babes-in-joyland approach served so frequently by Praise the Lord types is that as their resources increase and their influence extends, they will continue to promote an anemic, pabulum-coated gospel that passes for the real thing. The world can never be saved by Kool-Aid. Temporary refreshment does not take the place of a powerful discipleship that is alert and responsive to the tragedies of life and the opportunities for cosmic change that are the prompting of the Holy Spirit to wide-awake people.

I recall a Presbyterian minister in Long Island, New York, reporting on the history of his two-hundred-year-old congregation. It was created in precolonial times and survived the British occupation of that section of New York during the Revolutionary War. In fact, that particular community was at the center of several sharp engagements between British troops and Washington's men. The town suffered several evacuations, church services were suspended for long durations, and the smoke and noise of battle touched almost every corner of the tiny American village. My ministerial colleague said that he read the early records of the church, especially the official documents of the Session and their annual reports. The only mention of the entire Revolutionary War period with all of its commotion, anxiety, and danger swirling about that particular church was that, in currency, pounds were changed to dollars and people would make their tithes in the new style!

Without question, my solid impression of the Praise the Lord phenomenon of Christian motivation and outreach, is that prayer continues, Bible reading flourishes, tithes and offerings are generously promoted, but never a mention of civil rights, never a word about women's awareness, not one peep about a war in Southeast Asia, never a comment about the cancer of Watergate, and surely no acknowledgment that Israel and Egypt have anything to resolve in the Holy Lands. Without a whole gospel for the whole world, we have conversion for personal kicks and born-again people bent on entertainment and self-promotion. Let us never mistake the start for the finish, and Jesus is the finisher—the one who make things complete.

The success of Christianity can be seen quickly in its dealing with tragedy, sorrow, disaster, and moral calamity. Central is the willingness of Jesus to suffer for the sins of the whole world, the follies and failures of his closest followers, and the cruelties of Roman legal enforcement. The drama of life, death, and resurrection is offered to every believer and re-enacted in the sacrament of baptism. The shared cup and bread of Holy Communion becomes another major source of reminder and celebration that we belong to Christ and have a future as well as a past.

The principal figures in the born-again topic of our present era have all undergone significant suffering that, through their witness and testimony, has become almost public property. The power of a failure testimony—for that is what we have—only makes sense through the absolute honesty of the person speaking—leads us to understand the change wrought by the Holy Spirit, bringing the individual to a whole new level of existence that is traced to the life of Jesus. In theological technical terms, it really is a confession of faith and in reality is the bedrock of the New Testament writing.

• Peter's going to sleep during Jesus' crisis in the garden and his shameful denial, three times, the following early morning hours, would and could only come to us through his personal confession of such rotten behavior. Scriptures dare to recount this despicable cowardice because Peter was born again.

• Saul was a deliberate destroyer of the young Christian fellowship. He encouraged, with his approval, the stoning of Stephen and put dozens of believers into prison until he was confronted in a vision by the Risen Christ. The new Paul can admit to this sorry, destructive behavior because he was reclaimed, given a new creative life in the Spirit.

• Zacchaeus became the chief tax collector in Jericho for the Roman government. He was powerful and rich and was regarded as a traitor to Jewish traditions. When Jesus passes by, he climbs up to see him in a tree. Christ calls him down, invites himself into the house for lunch. Overwhelmed by the grace and forgiveness of Jesus, the despised Jewish tax authority states, during lunch, that he will give half of his wealth to the poor and "If I have defrauded any one of anything, I restore it fourfold." He was born again and took immediate steps to validate that conversion. "Today," said Jesus, "salvation has come to this house." (Luke 19:8–9)

THE PRODIGAL SON—THE FIRST BORN-AGAIN STORY

The church has always had difficulty with people who repent and return to the living fellowship with God. By church, I mean the established religious community that has cut the wood, carried the water, kept the lights on and the organ tuned. I mean the spiritual fellowship that has gathered year in and out, paid the bills, sent the missionaries, called on the sick and dying, worried about the future for young people, and seen that the pastor's pension dues were paid up—this crowd throughout all human history, at least a lot of them, have carried a natural resentment and envy against the born-again types who suddenly repent and are the toast of the apostles, disciples, and saints.

It is happening now and it was happening every time some notorious sinner heard clearly Jesus' message and decided to claim the new life promised in the Spirit. In fact, the strays were flocking to the prophet from Galilee in such throngs that people were murmuring against Jesus' success and he had to deal with the emotions of envy, resentment, and disgust that these feelings reflected.

So he told several stories as reported in Luke, where a shepherd has a hundred sheep, yet in discovering that one is lost, leaves the ninety-nine in the wilderness and starts searching for the lost one until he finds it. And when he does, he carries it back on his shoulders, for it may be exhausted or injured, and calls his neighbors saying, "Rejoice with me, for I have found my sheep which was lost." (Luke 15:3–7) Not only is the neighborhood happy, says Jesus, but, "there will be more joy in heaven over one sinner who repents than over ninety-nine righteous persons who need no repentance." (Luke 15:7)

Jesus' audience could appreciate the value in recovering the lost sheep. But what may have been really difficult to swallow was the story of the prodigal son who demanded that his father give him his part of the estate and raced off to another Las Vegas, squandering "his property in loose living. And when he had spent everything, a great famine arose in that country and he began to be in want."

There were no food stamps in those days and no such thing as unemployment insurance or disaster relief. You know the rest. The young man finally gets work herding swine—a real defeat for Jews who did not place keeping

pigs high on their priority list—and began to eat the vege-
tables that he was feeding them.

However, his head and his stomach are working over-
time and God often uses both to get our attention and
start the conversion process pumping. He resolves to return home and says to his father, "I have sinned against
heaven and you—I am no longer worthy to be called your
son—treat me as one of your hired servants." The lad is
hungry and humble and honest enough to admit it before
his father. That is a conversion experience, where repentance leads to true amendment of life.

The father is so joyful over his son's return that he runs
to greet him, embracing him in love and forgiveness and
calling his servants to bring a ring and a robe and some
shoes—all signs of honor and hospitality and acceptance
in Hebrew society. Not just an everyday welcome but a
real major open house. He was lost and was now found,
and the party of celebration began for everyone in the big
house with the pillars and the gravel driveway.

And then the resentment surfaces with smoke and fire.
The other son, an elder brother, is working in the fields
and hears the music with the barbecue aroma wafting
across the fields and the glasses tinkling and the laughter
and where-have-you-been-all-this-time shouts. Practically
a college homecoming for this first semester dropout.

And the elder son is so angry and disgusted that he re-
fuses his father's invitation to join in the banquet open
house, sharing a festivity with one who is burned out
from his loose living and harlot investing. And his father
reminds us succinctly:

> Son, you are always with me, and all that is mine is yours.
> It was fitting to make merry and be glad, for this your
> brother was dead and is alive; he was lost and is found."
> (Luke 15:31–32)

This illustration is being played again in most of the churches in North America. The notorious converts who spent their earlier days in criminal conduct, wild living, drugs and girls, and bad acting suddenly get all the fanfare, placed on the dais, and paid handsomely to tell thousands what a rotten life they have left behind. There is a solid and justified envy in the Christian ranks that these professional losers that tore up our society, threatened our government processes in Watergate, and had no regard or respect for the Christian cause are suddenly rich from their failures and honored for their infamy. It doesn't make sense, say many sitting in the pew or around the sewing circle, and those fund raising for a missionary society.

But let's face it right here; God's ways are not our ways. And the grace of God is not measured, controlled, or rationed by anyone in this world or his church. Let us also admit that all, including this writer, need forgiveness and reclamation every hour. Christians are not free from sin, they only know better than others that God forgives those who truly repent—seventy times seven. If the Christian community cannot find room to forgive not only its enemies, but its new members who are fresh in their penitence (while yes, they are banking already some of the rewards), then there is not a future in our faith and no point in reading further here. Perhaps what we can do and agree upon is a variety of styles and expressions in the reality of repentance.

ENLARGING THE JOYS AND FRUITS OF REPENTANCE

In the first of the early narratives of the book of Acts we have the excitement and energy of the young Christian church affecting a variety of persons with their surging good news. An Ethiopian, a eunuch who was the chief financial officer in the court of Queen Candace, had been in Jerusalem on a pilgrimage—probably to be part of the Passover celebration. One of the disciples, Philip, was led in the Spirit to travel the same road—from Jerusalem to Gaza. As he walked along, he joined himself to the Ethiopian's company and noted that the foreign visitor was reading from the prophet Isaiah. Philip offers to guide the Ethiopian in his study of the prophet, for he admits that he does not understand the Scripture.

Immediately Philip takes him through the fifty-third chapter of Isaiah, showing how it foresaw the suffering of Christ and how Jesus had just fulfilled this passage in his Easter morning resurrection. The traveler is convinced of the truth of the conversation with Jesus' follower and asks to be baptized, right there along the highway. It is accomplished and Philip vanishes and the Ethiopian goes on his way rejoicing. Christian tradition traces the thousands of years of Christian presence in that African state to this encounter with the Spirit of God along the road to Gaza.

What is important and different here is the readiness for affirmation of Christ's messiahship by one who had been faithful to God but not yet informed of the latest events. The Ethiopian was a man of integrity, commitment, and devotion. He was emotionally, psychologically, and spiritually ready to become a disciple of Jesus Christ. All he needed were the straight facts and a reliable teacher. When this fell into place along the Gaza road, mind and soul united to praise and glorify God in a new way—by becoming a complete Christian.

The baptism of the Ethiopian was not a sensational, public event. Only several were even aware of it, for it happened in isolation and certainly far removed from the type of conversion that Peter and Paul experienced. No uproar, no gossip, no headlines, no public rally or television coverage. Jesus had promised that the Kingdom of God would appear quietly and often silently. And he added that the Kingdom of God was within. It seems that this may be the norm for a religious experience for the majority of Christians. Life has its stars and skyrockets and Christianity has its parades and festivals, but most of us will come to know personally the love and presence of God in quiet moments, in solitary settings of the sanctuary of the soul.

During a twelve-month period I met and visited with Charles Colson, Eldridge Cleaver, and Tony Cox. Each of them had gone through a dramatic, life-changing conversion that had shaken trees and rattled windows. Their adventures were well known in the instance of Colson and Cleaver—and soon to be known in the story of Tony Cox and his years with the Beatles and Yoko Ono and his final victorious spiritual achievement in the life of Christ.

All the stories were dramatic, at times gasping and always related to the up-to-the-minute happenings found on the front page of your newspaper. Cox had been close to the center of the action, the entertainment province of the stardom ruled by the Beatles and Yoko. Cleaver had been and done everything wrong—crime, Black Muslims, Black Panthers, you name it. Colson had as many Watergate headlines as any other participant save Richard Nixon. They all were capable of drawing a crowd and, within the church, attracting appropriate publicity. But what about the invisible stars, the unknown champions who keep the Christian movement alive and well and wonderful?

Not long ago I went into my favorite department store,

J. C. Penney's. A decade ago I had become acquainted with the founder of that marvelous company and enjoyed working with Mr. Penney on a revision of one of his books. He was a radiant and thoughtful Christian, and his personality was not separate from the philosophy of his commercial enterprise.

I must admit, however, that I usually shop during big sales, attracted by the advertised specials that are good buys and represent legitimate value to the purchaser. The big, full-page ads had drawn me in to check things out. But while in the store, I noticed some unadvertised specials . . . a whole rack of jogging shorts. There were limitations as to color and size and style, but if you found the right combination and they had your size, it was a super buy.

I ended up not purchasing the shirts that were so gloriously promoted (and a legitimate end-of-season buy), but the unadvertised special—it had none of the publicity but has already given me complete satisfaction at a very cheap price.

I thought of the unadvertised special that I came to know this past year. The person had been a Christian for several years and suddenly, through a sharp crisis, needed to make a major remodeling of personal, family, and spiritual life. An angry, resentful, devious person became, through prayer, counseling, and love a radiant, loving, born-again Christian who salvaged a marriage, brought positive joy to a wide circle of friends, and continues to reflect the vitality and love of Jesus Christ. No publicity, no books or television appearances, no before-and-after dramatizations for a church convention—a real unadvertised special that tells us that the Christian life can be great and good—gently understated.

FINDING BALANCE IN THE BORN-AGAIN SURGE

We are always attracted to the lightning that dazzles the sky during a stormy night, but it is the quiet rain, not the thunderbolts that finally give nourishment to the earth. I don't want to see a diminution of the religious celebrities who brighten up our time—just an increase and appreciation for the other types who love Christ just as much but who will never gain the spotlight or applause.

Paul must have known all about this problem—and turned it into benefit for the whole Christian community. The early church thrived on the daring nerve and spiritual ingenuity and big splash that persons such as Paul and Peter accomplished in their world. They took on every kind of opposition and won The Jewish community put them down. The Romans were suspicious and finally lethal. The Greeks were sarcastic and cynical. The pagans were everywhere ignoring them. But these superstars prevailed; even though they gave their lives in the contest, the victory could be announced. But they still had this celebrity problem and it surfaced harshly in a new church at Corinth.

Some of the membership was attracted by the leadership of a man called Cephas. Others were impressed and convinced that a distinguished convert named Apollos was the real reason to get with the Christian cause. Others were dead certain that the Apostle Paul not only had the message but also a personal, life-changing vision of the Risen Christ. People let the discussion get out of hand in the church at Corinth. They became very unChristian in their appraisal of the other leaders' faults or deficiencies while lifting up their own hero. It was messy and pointless, but Paul has to deal with it and says,

> I appeal to you, brethren, by the name of our Lord Jesus Christ, that all of you agree and that there be no dissensions among you, but that you be united in the same mind and the same judgment. For it has been reported to me by Chloe's people that there is quarreling among you, my brethren. What I mean is that each one of you says, "I belong to Paul," . . . or "I belong to Cephas," or "I belong to Christ." Is Christ divided? Was Paul crucified for you? Or were you baptized in the name of Paul? (1 Cor. 1:10–13)

The Apostle was right all the way. People must avoid saying, "Well, Eldridge has got the gospel straight, not Colson." Or "Ruth Carter Stapleton has the right approach, much clearer than Dale Evans or Mark Hatfield." Christians can draw insight and strength from the whole crowd without subtracting from the witness any one. This problem has been around from the beginning—and will probably be there at the finals!

5

When the Glow Is Gone
and Getting It Back

An aspect of the spiritual life—even a requirement—which confronts every follower of Christ is to have remedies of renewal available when frustration sets in or defeats seem to be cracking the foundation of our personal faith.

Any meaningful recovery of spiritual strength will point us to our roots, to events and words and places far distant from the twentieth-century turf that is always pressing in —and often crowding out the soul.

How frequently and naturally Jesus spoke out of the Old Testament tradition. How honestly he could say that he came not to abolish the Law but fulfill it. Although Christians will always read the Old Testament through the eyes of a New Testament faith, the truths are waiting for us to reclaim and revalue.

When Jesus was asked to reply to a test question put to him by an ecclesiastical lawyer, a Pharisee, he gives a traditional answer—with a new twist that is important for our discussion. The question—which is the great commandment of the Law? The answer, without hesitation, Deuteronomy 6:4–5. For those not having a Bible handy, it reads,

Hear, O Israel: The LORD our God is one LORD; And you shall love the LORD your God with all your heart, and with all your soul, and with all your might.

While he quoted directly from the Old Testament book of the Law, Deuteronomy, Jesus did make one small but powerful change, and it was in the last phrase, reported in the twenty-second chapter of Matthew:

> You shall love the Lord your God with all your heart, with all your soul, and with all your *mind*. (Matt. 22:37)

Jesus added the intellectual component as one of the key ways that we can honor and love God. Through the powers of the intelligent inquiry, through the gifts of creative questions and sincere probing, the will of God is revealed to our time. That is a significant part of our Christian heritage. It is also a style that can be passed from one generation to another.

When we ponder other powerful Christian leaders in the young New Testament church, we discover that several of them did not arrive at a meaningful faith through a cataclysmic conversion. Consider Timothy. Next to Paul he may have been the leading evangelist and apologist of the early church. He was young and bright and daring— and at times pretty pushy. Yet Paul feels him not only to be his natural successor in matters of the faith but regards him as "my true child in the faith." (1 Tim. 1:2) In other places he says, "This charge I commit to you, Timothy, my son, in accordance with the prophetic utterances which pointed to you, that inspired by them you may wage the good warfare, holding faith and a good conscience." (1 Tim. 1:18)

Timothy had been marked early for advance work in the Kingdom of God. His confession of faith must have come at the time of high school and it was given "in the presence of many witnesses." Paul then gives us a clue concerning the spiritual lineage of Timothy's household:

> I thank God whom I serve with a clear conscience, as did my fathers, when I remember you constantly in my prayers. As I remember your tears, I long night and day

to see you, that I may be filled with joy. I am reminded of your sincere faith, a faith that dwelt first in your grandmother Lois and your mother Eunice and now, I am sure, dwells in you. Hence I remind you to rekindle the gift of God that is within you. . . . (2 Tim. 1:3–6)

There is a hint in Paul's second letter to his young associate in Christ that Timothy had backed off from his initial enthusiasm and church leadership. Other information from the epistles indicate there had been some differences in strategy or expectation, with Timothy returning prematurely from a missionary journey. Whatever, Paul is suggesting that the embers and glow of faith need only to be rekindled and the enthusiasm and excitement will return stronger than ever.

That is sound advice for more than a young Christian two thousand years ago. Kierkegaard asked the same question in another century: How do you become a Christian when you already are one? How do you become a Christian all over again, when the Gospel seems stale, the fellowship is flagging, and the personal zeal has touched a low level? Prayer is the secret. Paul remembered Timothy constantly in his prayers.

And finally a Christian of our day and age, John Killinger, the author of *Bread for the Wilderness, Wine for the Journey*, reflects on the vibrant faith that operated so freely in his young life and then waned and was nearly snuffed out. But through the power of prayer an amazing, positive spiritual recovery established itself. Looking at the whole life story, his own, John Killinger may be telling yours as well:

There was a time when I saw it very clearly. It was during my adolescence. I lived like young Wordsworth, with "intimations of immortality" all around me. I lived, breathed, slept with a sense of the presence of God.

Every bush was a burning bush, every creek a sacred stream. Once I saw an angel, bright as the sun, diaphanous as a movie projection. There was no question of its reality . . . the vision was a gift, as life itself was. I saw with a single eye.

He continues,

Then the world began to wean me away from belief in Angels. Not suddenly or dramatically, but gradually. I became caught up in its frantic pace. I learned to speak the language of its jaunty secularism and self-assurance. I submitted to its subtle way of psychologizing everything about me—my dreams, my loves, even my beliefs.

Then Killinger, like a theological dentist, touches that exposed nerve that is so frequent, too common, ever happening in our personal lives:

The enthusiasm, the fire that had burned inside me, actually damped. The living flame became a hidden coal. I have warmed myself at that coal for years. It has kept me going, through college and seminary, marriage, career, parenthood. Now I want it to flame out again, to burn freely and wildly, and joyously the way it once did. I want it to consume me again. And there are signs that it is going to . . .

I can only say that Killinger is right. Prayer is the answer. It is right and correct because it works and has happened that way with me.

Several years ago I was working in an executive job for the United Presbyterian Church in the Southwest. I had been nearly a decade in religious publishing in New York and thought that I would probably spend the rest of my ministry in the realm of writing, missionary interpretation, and fund raising for church causes.

When the First Presbyterian Church in Albuquerque

was seeking a new senior pastor, I felt flattered when a friend proposed my name. Little did I really expect to be in the final consideration of the Pastor Seeking Committee, and how stunned I felt the day I learned that my name had become their first choice as pastor of this great western congregation.

Flattery turned to fear. I had not served as a parish pastor for more than ten years. I dreaded the tensions and conflicts that were natural to energetic congregations. But more than the executive/personnel demands of leading a thirty-person staff of a 2,500-member church, I knew myself to be spiritually at zero. My prayer life was anemic and, at times, nonexistent. The Scriptures were friendly but not foremost in my studies. My faith seemed like a middle-aged car with a flat tire, the motor was racing but there was no means to move.

I was literally driven to my knees and began to say with urgency and despair, O Lord, if this is your will, let your strength replace my weakness; let your way direct my will; let your Son Jesus come again into this frail soul, that I may not falter in doing your work.

Something began to happen. Instead of avoiding quiet moments of meditation and prayer, I began to enlarge the time and extend the concerns. I began to pray for others with a new expectation and zest. I felt lifted and supported by a power that had never been resident in my life. My anxiety about conflict and my dread of congregational infighting vanished. I was living on faith, by faith in the Son of the Living God. I felt my life and ministry to be owned by Paul's words: "God did not give us a spirit of timidity, but a spirit of power and love and self-control." (2 Tim. 1:7) That was my theme without knowing it, and it may be your slogan for the life that is lasting and triumphant.

Most of us are weak, vacillating Christians. We surge and sigh, we march bravely and then know the dread of collapse and failure. Our faith needs rekindling and it comes only when we open our lives up in prayer and are also willing to share our disabilities and disasters with others. Emerson once wrote in his journal: "'Tis bad when believers and unbelievers live in the same manner—I distrust religion." So should we if our lives do not reflect the great possibilities of the Gospel and the living promises offered by Jesus to his faithful followers. If the Christian enterprise is not built on prayer, it really differs only slightly from the other visible establishments in our world.

Here are six suggestions for rekindling your faith through prayer.

1. Pray without ceasing. That was St. Paul's guideline. There is not a person, problem, opportunity, or situation that is not aided by prayer. Few of us can be in constant, verbal petition to Almighty God. Yet we can develop a prayer picture that includes everyone we meet and everything we must accomplish.

2. Pray specifically. Jesus taught his disciples to pray—at their request. When you study and pray the Lord's Prayer, you realize how practical and specific your prayers should be. Jesus started and directed his prayer to the source of all life. He said, "Our Father." That brings us to the central power of the universe, which in prayer we know is both personal and present. This kind of true prayer draws us away from self and lifts us by the power of the Spirit to the grace of God and his will.

3. Mention concerns, people, problems by name. Many friends keep a daily prayer list. They reach out in love and compassion for the world's hungry, for the victims of war, for the sick and the dying. They also pray

thankfully for spring rain and a startling sunset. Their prayers, drawn out of the deep well of human compassion and agape love, are praying in and with the will of God. Such prayers become life, and it is a life with God that will never end.

4. Pray with periods of quiet and expectant listening. We need not always be in the presence of God with an urgent, demanding shopping list. We can be still and know that thou art God, says the Psalmist. In return rest shall be your strength. Find a quiet, solitary place to pray alone. Be in a comfortable position. Stick around a while. The life of prayer is worth everything, even a place on our schedule, for soon it will rearrange the priorities of our days.

5. Learn the Jesus Prayer: Lord Jesus Christ
                              Son of God
                              Have Mercy on Me, a Sinner.
This ancient prayer, which may be used effectively as we breathe the air in and out of our lungs, gives our vision a whole new focus on the person of Jesus the Christ.

6. Pray with confidence and trust. The saints have always believed that the Holy Spirit intercedes for us "with sighs too deep for words." God's caring, sustaining force finds fresh openings in the lives of prayer. Paul said, "Have no anxiety about anything, but in everything by prayer and supplication with thanksgiving let your requests be made known to God. And the peace of God, which passes all understanding will keep your hearts and minds in Christ Jesus." (Phil. 4:6–7) The Apostle found the divine formula—our anxiety, despair, and worry loses its hold when Christ Jesus is in our hearts.

The major understanding that most Christian people need to incorporate into their positive life style, and a result of the "rekindling" of their spiritual strength, is that

they can cope with the catastrophes of life—for they will
have their share with or without a born-again episode. As
Cecil Osborne emphatically summarizes in his *The Art of
Becoming a Whole Person:*

> One may be living a dedicated Christian life and still ex-
> perience such things as an impaired marriage, physical
> illness, bankruptcy, death of a loved one, the loss of
> friends, and other major or minor disasters.
> I have known splendid Christians who tithed and later
> went bankrupt; devoted Christian workers who had men-
> tal breakdowns; ministers who were subject to fits of
> deepest depression, Sunday school teachers whose chil-
> dren committed suicide. Being a Christian is no guaran-
> tee of success in business nor does it guarantee freedom
> from sickness, sorrow, or failure. . . . What Christ does
> offer us is strength to overcome, to win out in the end, to
> withstand whatever happens to us.

Our reasoning processes and our rational skills must in-
form us always that no mature spiritual state is going to
exist for Christians that is absent or free from difficulty
and mishap. When we look again at the life of Christ, we
witness an arena of bitter suffering and the ultimate in-
dignity of a public execution. We see disciples stoned,
apostles imprisoned, and martyrs destroyed. The Christian life is a great life because it can endure, not because
it cops out or is immune to the sinful behavior of others.
St. Paul put it on the line for generations to follow by
when considering their plight:

> We are afflicted in every way, but not crushed; perplexed,
> but not driven to despair; persecuted but not forsaken;
> struck down but not destroyed; always carrying in the
> body the death of Jesus, so that the life of Jesus may be
> manifested in our bodies. . . . So death is at work in us,
> but life in you. (2 Cor. 4:8–10, 12)

WHEN THE GLOW IS GONE AND GETTING IT BACK

When you consider the great variety of personal, intimate commitments that one must make in life, it is not surprising that a time comes that these intentions are tested and found wanting. We make big investments in education, and we follow stimulating pursuits in the business, professional, and employment world; the attractions of romance lead us to marriage and the compelling call of Jesus Christ directs us to find expression and life in the Christian church. Yet each one of these commitments can falter, stumble, and fail. It is a fact of life, a root of reality that every one of our intense, personal goals has low levels of satisfaction and deep periods of blockage and failure.

We are especially chagrined when this condition afflicts our marriage or our career—we are distraught when it erodes our Christian affirmation and we silently confess that the glow is gone. Of all recent writers and persons I have known, Jeb Magruder seems to be most disarmingly candid on this topic. He can't resist leveling when he says, "It seemed to me that meeting Christ was one thing, and learning how to live his way was another, and you couldn't accomplish both in a matter of a few minutes."

Magruder went on to say that his schedule as a new Christian convert took him on the Christian banquet circuit where he was to meet all kind of born-again personalities. They had become famous celebrities with smooth spiritual routines—yet many shocked him by their cynical asides and developing self-doubts. Several confided that they thought their new experience in Christ would be a deeper, more abiding experience, and now they recognized that they were living on the surface and their newly gained faith was getting shaky.

Should this surprise us, really? A youngster goes away to college, and the first few weeks are pure sensation. Lots of independence and freedom, exhilarating moments of entertainment and campus glamour. And then the grind sets in and classes become heavy and papers are announced and midterm exams loom up like a thunderstorm. And that swell roommate has started to borrow money and clothes and class notes, and the people down the hall can't find the volume control on the stereo, and the groovy course of study turns out to be a form of intellectual entrapment, and yes, the glow has gone so swiftly.

I don't need to summarize but remind you that this is the arrangement of life; this is one of its severe realities. André Gide told us rightly that "everything that needs to be said has already been said. But since no one was listening, everything must be said again." And so the glow flickers in our employment and professional choices. And the glow fades in our marriage, and we admit that the romance is gone and the grind has started: it usually starts with money or sex and then expands to include the family, the choice of pets, and the poor selection of friends, hobbies, sports, or religion. But the central theme is never examined soon enough—that our lives are saturated with selfishness and our consumer style of life has deeply infected our marriage, which requires giving, not getting. And if the fading dreams can collapse college and marriage and professional pursuits, they can also settle in forever on our Christian commitments and turn the flame of faith into an almost dying spark.

It's not always our fault, not always. Just when we were looking for strength, guidance, and support with the Christian fellowship, we were stricken with a group of small minds and petty participants. They can swarm in any given church at any moment; and when they surround the joy and enthusiasm of a new believer, they can almost stifle the high hopes of a true faith.

But it is deeper and more dangerous than that. It is usually our personal failure as a new Christian (of any age) to be rooted and grounded in a living faith that is truly in touch with God and fellow believers. Some years ago I was serving on a college board of trustees with Colleen Townsend Evans, a promising Hollywood starlet who had given up a career in the movies to find a more dynamic role in the wider Christian community. She had become noted for her celebrity conversion and through the years was a sought-after personality at church conventions, laity conferences, and evangelical assemblies. We served on several committees together and what impressed me was the considerate, open approach that she had with other people. The Student Relations Committee (of this college board) was not an easy assignment; in fact, it was one often filled with topics and disagreements that could be sharply controversial. Yet Mrs. Evans never faltered in her genuine exchange with young people of opposing, even conflicting values and radiated a natural, contagious human caring. Her Christian notoriety had taken a new channel, was finding fresh avenues of expression and exposure.

Some time earlier a person in my congregation had given me a copy of her book, *A New Joy*. It was there that she revealed the same anxiety that Jeb Magruder acknowledged (and quotes in his book) and how she had to deal with this sensation of waking one morning and discovering that the glow of faith was gone.

For several years before I married Louie, I had worked in the motion picture industry. . . [T]o many people the combination of my belief and my profession had a special attraction . . . even after I left my motion picture work for my "other career," the one I wanted more, the speaking invitations continued. . . . I said yes to as many requests as I could, although speaking was not then (and is not now) a thing I leap toward with joy. Eventually the pressure became uncomfortable because I allowed myself to be influenced by a few people who felt that it was not only my opportunity but my duty to speak about Jesus publicly.

Yes, I could see where the glow had gone. It had retreated deep inside me. . . . [I]t is one thing to talk about being a Christian in front of groups, but quite another to be a Christian in your home and in your community.

Colleen at last was able to find the sustaining power of her faith in the closer, more realistic expressions of her personal life—with her family, the people of her neighborhood, and the members of her home church.

The point is essential and well taken—the glow of a lifting, enriching, zestful Christian experience can seem to evaporate or diminish or vanish. It really has gone inside of us, waiting for genuine expression and true growth experiences. Jesus said that it had to take root. Paul said that when we are rooted and grounded in love, nothing can prevail against us. The Christian life can never lie fallow for long—it either expands or dies.

One aspect of the spiritual life that confronts every follower of Christ is to have remedies of renewal available when frustration sets in or defeats seem to be cracking the foundation of our personal faith.

To be a Christian is to be a risk-taking person, for there are costs and commitments to be fulfilled and adventures taken. Not long ago several of my Albuquerque neighbors successfully completed the first trans-Atlantic crossing in a balloon. The flight of the Double Eagle II is now history, but our community still thrills to the stunning accounts of this six-day crossing of the Atlantic Ocean.

From the very beginning the hazards of flight were prominent—the balloon during lift-off from Presque Isle, Maine, narrowly missed some treacherous power lines. Several days out, the flyers navigated through a vigorous cold front that iced the top of their balloon and then saw them plunge twenty thousand feet in less than five minutes. Their final landing in France brought world acclaim —and civic pride to Albuquerque.

What sticks in my memory was not the successful flight of 1978, but the failure of their first flight in September 1977. One crew member, Ben Abruzzo, said that they were not prepared on the initial try for the sudden adverse weather, the drenching rain, the bone-cold hours of exposure in an open gondola, the final torment of being caught in an Atlantic storm off the coast of Greenland and nearly out of touch with radio trackers.

When Abruzzo reviewed the first attempt for a civic club, he said flatly that he would never again attempt such a balloon flight The shocking memories of ditching in the waters off Greenland, the uncontrollable forces of weather, wind, and ocean, the hanging on for rescue— never, never, never again would he be part of such a risk.

And what do we say when a person backs away from a challenge, a job, a tournament, a task they no longer find fulfilling or rewarding? We say that they lose heart, or that their heart is not in it And this is true not only of the big, visible adventures like an ocean crossing or a mountain ascent—but in the daily tasks where life really makes or breaks us. In our work, our hobbies, our marriages— and especially in our Christian affirmations—we find to our dismay, that at times, our heart is not in it, and we verge on the point of failure.

One of the reasons that we lose heart—followed by a loss of zest and exuberance—is that our original resolution was not grounded in Christ and did not find fulfillment in loving expression. We may have come to a decision or commitment that was out of hope for personal advantage or some aspect of self-indulgence or self-interest.

While considering this dilemma, I came across the observation that a writer made concerning F. Scott Fitzgerald, the literary commentator of the Roaring Twenties. Fitzgerald was to gain incredible fame and success as a writer and then suffer incredible collapse, even before reaching middle age. During the twilight of his professional career, Fitzgerald spent a summer in Asheville, North Carolina, in 1935. He befriended a young bookstore proprietor and shared many afternoons in conversation and comment. The famous writer was wrestling with alcoholism and the crack-up of his marriage. Both factors were preying on his writing talent, and he noted "that it is impossible to write without hope."

When his bookstore pal asked if he were still corresponding with a New York City sweetheart, he replied that a note of bitterness had crept into Rosemary's letters —she believed that Fitzgerald had forgotten her—and he was now fearful that she remembered his crushing comment that "relationships like everything else, had an unfortunate way of wearing out."

If Christians are to overcome the validity of that statement, it will be through the exercise of day-to-day events that renew and revive the spirit within, by the Holy Spirit from above. The greatest single strength of any person's life is the relationships that share our deepest concerns. The earliest Christian communities in the New Testament thrived on fellowship, prayer, worship, and service. None of these can be bypassed today. No Christian enterprise in the future can last without them. Personal prayer and Bible study are just as vital as public times of praise and worship. There is a circuit that connects the two, and it must be honored and developed.

I don't believe that it is inaccurate to state that the Bible not only gives us the truth of our faith—but the technique to practice it as well. Some time ago I came across the fine little book *The Greatest Thing in the World* by Henry Drummond. It is an enduring Christian classic, and the author centers his big pitch on our attention to love in all its fullness and grace. His specific passage is Paul's letter to the Corinthians, chapter 13: "Faith, hope, love abide, these three, but the greatest of these is love." (1 Cor. 13:13)

Drummond was not only a scholar, Christian lay preacher, and biological scientist—he was also a devotional helper to millions. He proposes that no person can read this chapter 13 for every day of a month and not be a different, better, more fulfilled Christian.

Those who have accepted his challenge bear witness to the truth of this passage of Scripture. Not long ago I was visiting with a business friend in a southwestern city. He was successful in secular affairs—almost too much so, for his private life was saturated with a blunt, hard-driving brutality that hurt people and made relationships trying and abbreviated. I mentioned to him, during a time of sharing and discussion, this directive from Henry Drummond. Almost instantly he said, "I'll try it. I need something to turn my life around." The changes were nothing less than amazing. He not only read First Epistle to the Corinthians, chapter 13, every day, but finally memorized the entire chapter, discovering that the power of the Word and words can vitally change lives—our own.

In her book *The Experience of Inner Healing*, Ruth Carter Stapleton identifies the directions that have been successful for her in the realm of Christian care and growth. She suggests that as we enter the deep channel of caring and service, we at last discover the depths of God's presence—and the opportunity for vital renewal.

> There is fulfillment in serving others which nothing else can bring, there is a beauty in people hidden from the unconcerned or the merely curious.

The graciousness of visiting the sick, the risk of seeking out those in prison because you care, the bearing of another's burden, whether it be in sorrow or social disgrace, these are the quiet acts of serving ready to be incorporated into our lives as growing Christians. When they are neglected through disinterest, ignorance, or busyness, our responsiveness sags and worse, so does the soul within. As Ruth Stapleton writes,

> Only the caring can enter the rich inner sanctum of another. When one comes with the quiet listening spirit committed to unconditional love, the image of God appears in another, even through the shadows of an imperfect heart. The cynic sees only the imperfections, and therefore sees humanity as deserving destruction. Jesus sees through the imperfections to the image of God, and so he loved all of us enough to do so we might live. We see less clearly than he. But when we give our lives to others, we catch glimpses, we have visionary moments, when plain and broken people reveal their beauty and make our lives beautiful.

When things aren't working, in any segment of life, it usually means that we require the help of others—and we should ask for it. When a tooth hurts or a back aches or an eye flares up, we go instantly for professional guidance. This is true of the life of the spirit. We should not put off or postpone our call for help.

Some years ago our family bought a fine young Arab gelding from a breeder, who also provided the initial training. We rode the horse on his grounds, as we continued to keep him at his original home until we could locate a stable closer to our home. After six months we shifted the animal and established him in a fine new location not far from where we lived. Everything seemed to go wrong. . . . Almost like a sudden case of nerves or homesickness. "Amigo" stopped eating and acted as if the alfalfa were poison. On the riding trails he became apprehensive and spooky. In the arena where we worked him daily for development and further training, he fought our leads and discovered that he enjoyed bucking. It was trying and even tormenting, for we thought of ourselves as advanced riders. Finally we called in our professional friend. He spurred the animal a couple of times, talked to him, and in less than it takes to describe, had drained out the spookiness and edginess of the young horse. It was back to basics, back to firm direction and control, it was being consistent and firm and a skittish horse became a fairground winner.

Christians have to be in touch with each other to be reminded of the basics, to remember how they work, and to see someone else giving guidance and comfort and hope. It does require humility and honesty on our part to reach out for help, especially when we consider ourselves advanced and expert in religious matters. But I think of Edith Wade and her great victory at Wimbledon, coming late in her professional career after missing the big trophy for so many years. She finally admitted she needed help, as a top-flight world cup professional and found it in a California teacher who helped her to go the one stride further and master her emotions as well as extend her great talent. She won at last because she was shattered enough to seek assistance and direction from another.

Anyone serious about personal revitalization of faith is going to focus his or her mind as well as actions on the claims of Jesus Christ. Ruth Stapleton argues that just as our bodies require proper nourishment and exercise, so do our minds. The emotional health and spiritual well-being of each one of us is measured by the input—the feeding that our intellect receives daily. Her suggestions are essential to the health of vital Christianity:

> We sometimes neglect our responsibility to fill our minds with the good and the beautiful rather than the ugly, the trashy, and the unworthy. . . . Those who fill their minds with the thoughts of love for God and others, who learn to smile so that others may be happy without intending to impress others with their humor or piety, are quietly building a storehouse of blessing which will enable them to hear and heed the voice of God.

Mrs. Stapleton went on to add some practical aids for persons seeking to enlarge the capacity of soul and the generous heart. She recalled a suggested discipline that we all can follow—to vanquish negative and destructive and depressing thoughts by incorporating a "spiritual fast." The process was simple but profound—the technique was to have a seven-day fast from negative thoughts by supplanting such moods and ideas with positive input. And one of the positive portions of the New Testament is employed:

> Whatever is true, whatever is honorable, whatever is just, whatever is pure, whatever is lovely, whatever is gra-

cious, if there is any excellence, if there is anything
worthy of praise, think about these things. . . . [A]nd the
God of peace will be with you. (Phil. 4:8–9)

This may seem corny or play-school to some, but to this
writer, it is dynamite. We all profit from filling our lives
with the integrity and power of biblical truth. It expands
and extends its influence through deployment—in us. And
it works. Henri Nouwen reports that he now believes, as a
Christian person, that he has been able to memorize and
incorporate enough Scripture to deal with the stress and
pain of life. Scripture is that way—it seeks a home in us
and when that develops, life changes dramatically and
hopefully.

6

Where Christ Is Found—
In Individuals or Institutions

On the Mount of Transfiguration, Peter is prepared to build a monument preserving the vision revealed to him. He wants to preserve, isolate, freeze, reserve, and protect one of the truly holy moments in a person's life. So does every born-again personality today.

Peter, James, and John accompanied Jesus on a needed rest away from the crowd. As he frequently did for renewal and time off, Jesus went to the mountains. It was cool and private and distant from the increasing throngs that were attracted in a popular way to his preaching. Mark records that Jesus

> led them up a high mountain apart by themselves and he was transfigured before them, and his garments became glistening, intensely white, as no fuller on earth could bleach them. And there appeared to them Elijah with Moses; and they were talking to Jesus. (Mark 9:2–4)

If we had no Easter story, no resurrection account in the life of Jesus, this one event would have enough potential power to alter the shape of Hebrew religion and establish for believers the authenticity of the Messiahship of Jesus Christ.

Moses and Elijah were talking with Jesus. (Luke enlarges the experience in his account to say that Jesus was in prayer when this event took place. Matthew omits the prayer possibility and says that Jesus' face "shone like the sun and his garments became white as light." Matt. 17:2) The greatest of the lawgivers and, certainly, the founder

of this Holy Nation: Moses; and Elijah, the greatest of
the prophets, who was accounted as having resurrection
powers—both in the spiritual company with Christ and
how cosmic a meeting of the three servants of Almighty
God.

Peter, the activist and the realist, is not totally silenced
by this awesome revelation that no one in Creation has
ever observed. He says to Jesus, it is good that we are
here and witnessed this amazing moment. Let us build
three booths here—one for each of you, that this sacred
hour can be captured and honored by God's people
through all time. Peter sounds like Solomon, prepared to
build a temple for the Commandments and the Worship
of a Holy Nation. Perhaps this is the new Jerusalem, for
here are the giants of revealed religion, and this will be a
site that is irresistible to all mankind for all time to come.
Peter may be an aggressive, robust fisherman, but in this
flashing instance he sounds like the Frank Lloyd Wright
of religion. He is like you and me—he wants to preserve,
isolate, freeze, reserve, and protect one of the truly holy
moments in a person's life—and give others a chance to
share in its marvel and might.

But a voice from heaven—out of the clouds—fairly
shouts at the disciples, "This is my Son, listen to him."
And Jesus tells Peter and James and John that they are to
keep this happening a secret until after the Resurrection.
With bewildered steps and head-shaking sighs, the
witnesses follow Jesus down the mountain to the plain.

God's ways are not our ways and his Spirit restrains the
rush for sacred building and holy grounds—choosing to
have us find the divine in the commonplace, like a burning bush for Moses and a baby's cry for Joseph. God is
saying I am interested in the matters of the heart, the attitude of your soul, the sanctuary of your spirit. There I

would be known and reverenced and worshipped. Look for the increase of inner person; press on the enlargement of your soul. And listen to my Son as you get off this mountain, bringing fresh signs of the Kingdom of God to lives of people.

And that is both our problem and our potential: our problem is the yearning and desire to rest joyously in today's revelation by God, saying, Lord this is the high point; it is good that we are here to organize and institutionalize this sacred hour. And God keeps pushing us on, resisting our caution, which flows finally into a religious conservatism that forgets the new and wondrous things happening every day and will happen tomorrow.

This is a particular stress point for every one who has had a thrilling, unique born-again experience—how to praise God for the exhilaration and release of that powerful, loving, lifting event—and how to go on and not freeze that into some distorted, out-of-touch happening in our total human achievement. I remember visiting with Eldridge Cleaver one afternoon in Santa Fe, New Mexico, when we were putting the finishing touches to his new book *Soul on Fire*. I asked him what he would be talking about, for he was to speak shortly at a major church convention in the Southwest. He replied, "I suppose I will talk about my conversion, give my testimony. That's what people want to hear. But you know, I'm getting tired of just speaking on that—I want to add other experiences that are going on right now."

I wondered if that were not a universal feeling among people—not just those who have been through a glorious revelation of religious uplift. I wonder if Glen Campbell doesn't, finally, get weary of the requests to sing "Wichita Lineman" and Jim Fixx may want to be on a talk show that has more questions than just about running and marathons, and maybe Anita Bryant would like some other theme besides homosexuality. This weariness seems to be a special curse for athletes, especially in the professional ranks. I mean, a person can do other things besides catch a pass in the Super Bowl or win the British Open. But for the nonachievers, these are skyscraper experiences, and the gee-whiz quality never tires, for them, in the telling.

Jeb Stuart Magruder, one of the Watergate participants and later one of its victims, writes a rather stirring story in his spiritual pilgrimage described in *From Power to Peace*. He identifies the persons who helped him recover the whole picture of life and the special role of Christ for his forgiveness and recovery. His skill at writing and his winsome style of speaking opened a vast Christian audience to share in his conversion—his rebirth. But the routine and requirements of such a Christian celebrity circuit began to wear thin: the incessant travel, the boxing style of the press, which always wanted to question his motives for finding Christ and his surprising change in behavior. He knew he had skills that could be fulfilled in Christian work, but the banquet-television circuit did not seem to be the place. And then there was a deep inner reserve he had about the replay of his religious moment:

> Jesus Christ has changed my life, but that change is still going on, and hopefully will continue for the rest of my life. He turned me in a new direction, but I don't believe he intends me to stand in one spot along the way. He wants me to move ahead.

Then Magruder touched the center of this problem, for him and for every other person who is up front in the Christian conversion business when he added,

> I have a testimony to give and I want to most earnestly give it. But I don't want to make a career of it or allow

that to become my entire Christian experience. The moment when I met Christ was the beginning of my life, and the rest of that life now has to be lived out as Christ chooses.

When I talk about the moment I met Christ I am referring to the past—which is itself all right. But to speak over and over about a moment in the past prevents me from moving on into the future—and that is where I must go.

One of the critical questions faced by the most successful of the Christian personalities who have had enormous fame and fortune flow in their direction is just what to do with all that cash. Oral Roberts has built a staggering enterprise in Tulsa, Oklahoma, initiated by his early healing services that started in a tent with one-night stands. This extended significantly through radio and television, reaching an amazing number of individuals who believed that Roberts was able to bring them health, wholeness, and recovery.

In more recent years, the pentecostal nature of Roberts' ministry has been channeled into a more traditional, independent ministry, encompassing a university and lately an important medical school and hospital. The cash flow for such a dream is staggering. Millions upon millions of dollars are creating this program, which started from a man in overalls, pleading and praying for the healing of persons in his audience. Roberts himself has moved theologically and socially to the center of the Christian community—himself being enrolled as a member of the Methodist clergy. What does this tell us but that there are countless people who need special attention from the Christian family and have found it nowhere else but in the preaching, healing proclamations of Oral Roberts.

Now the intensity of the earlier tent days has been

refined and presented in slick, widely syndicated television specials, which bring a southwestern flavor to the wider viewing audience. Celebrity Christian guests are important to the format of the program, and the Roberts ministry is now firmly established within the hierarchy of his family and the big campus development in Tulsa. Roberts has the cordiality of a successful businessman and the vision of a concerned Christian who has significantly widened the initial thrust of his gospel tent preaching and healing.

Billy Graham's success publicly is even more extensive than Roberts but without the centering down, up to now, of an institution to define his mission and become the focus of his resources. Graham's major advance for Christian evangelism is the unbreakable rule of being sponsored by local Christian bodies in cities where his Crusade appears. His Crusades overseas have also followed this pattern, reflecting a broad ecumenical base before starting a preaching mission. Much of the monies collected by the Crusade offerings have gone back into those cities to pay for the expenses of the program and the training of the participants.

The additional offerings generated by mass television programming and the abundant readership of *Decision* magazine have helped to swell the annual income of the Billy Graham Evangelistic Association to $28.7 million. All of these illustrations—as well as the announced multimillion Holovita Center being proposed by Ruth Carter Stapleton for Texas, with lodging, recreation, theater, arts and crafts, and therapy—are natural outlets for people with vision, drive, and money.

The greatest difficulty may be seen in several tangents —the first is that our nation is facing a staggering tax problem with untold billions of dollars of real estate sheltered by education, religious, and nonprofit organizations. This free ride is meant to protect the freedom of religion and to advance the common life through nonprofit, charitable societies. However, persons like Reverend Moon have shown us how skillfully one can build a Unification Church through the pyramiding of real estate in New York and Westchester and shelter the grand total under the nonprofit exemption. What the benefits of this sort of operation are, I leave for the public to decide.

So many of the born-again personalities are creating nonprofit corporations (to assist in the tax break for the donor and the tax relief of the recipients) that some new guidelines must appear for the integrity of the Christian Gospel and the assistance to a society being badly squeezed under our present tax distribution.

Some of the more concerned, socially aware religious organizations are making contributions to local tax agencies to pay an appropriate amount of money, voluntarily, to assist the schools, highways, and social agencies that serve us all. If these gestures are not more widely followed and increased, the religious power of property and money is going to be a glaring judgment on the church and may result in a revision of tax laws that will not be welcome by anyone in charitable service today.

Even as we consider this difficulty I am reminded of Mark Hatfield's assertion that government is not always the answer and that religious groups do have a special calling that no one else can fulfill. A tax break for nonprofits does provide particular assistance. Said Hatfield,

> Government is limited in its priorities in a way which the Christian church is not. The greatest commandment we have is to love God and to love our neighbors. And love is not an emotion. It is action. . . . [W]e should not totally

abdicate this work to agencies which do not have the underpinning of love and motivation of Jesus Christ.

HOW TO TELL OTHER PEOPLE

A natural result of a conversion event is the born-again individual's eagerness to tell other people. This is a prevailing pattern throughout the New Testament and on through the ages of church history. When Andrew heard John the Baptist call Jesus the Lamb of God, he told his brother Simon Peter that the Messiah had been found. When Philip responded to the direct invitation to be a follower, he immediately went to his brother, Nathaniel, and said, "We have found him of whom Moses in the law and also the prophets wrote." Brothers were telling brothers. In Paul's letter to the Thessalonians, he reminds them that they have brought so much hope and joy in his life because "You became an example to all the believers in Macedonia and in Achaia. . . . [N]ot only has the word of the Lord sounded forth from you . . . but your faith in God has gone forth everywhere. . . ." (1 Thess. 1:7–8)

The Christian conversation and proclamation is the great thing that God has done in Christ—for you and me. If it is not contagious and personal, it may be concluded that it really is not Christian, for this is the whole impulse of the good news: that others might share in the liberation and joy.

There are many different expressions and strategies and ministries that are identified with present-day born-again personalities. Chuck Colson is pursuing a prison ministry, in conjunction with others called Fellowship House in

Washington, D.C. Eldridge Cleaver has incorporated an operation called Cleaver Crusades, with offices in Los Angeles and Stanford, California. His stationery has a logo of three crosses, which Eldridge describes as "His cross, your cross, and my cross." Already his organization has developed mailings inviting donors to support with cash gifts and prayers his work among the disadvantaged as well as the young people struggling in slum areas. Like Ruth Carter Stapleton, he would like to have a ranch operation in Texas. The Crusades, led by Eldridge, are a mixture of song and praise and speaking by Cleaver, sponsored by a local congregation or church groups, such as Full Gospel business outfits. Witness, testimony, and circuit appearances seem to be the expected formula for men and women who have had a vivid encounter with God in the life-changing way. Then larger audiences are achieved by taking it on the road or through television.

What has emerged is a particular popular style of presenting the Gospel through a form of ministry linked with evangelism and accompanying forms of theology, worship, music, and prayer. It is essentially conservative and, in some instances, can nearly be anti-intellectual. Simply stated, the impact is this: since I have had a life-changing, born-again encounter, my faith is complete, my theology established, and my message absolute. If that begins to pass, in the popular mind, as the fulfillment or final essence of the Christian life, we are in deep trouble.

Fortunately, several have been wise to catch this temptation right at the start and identify its misuse of people and the faith. Said Jeb Magruder,

> I could speak publicly if I had to, and I had done a great deal of it in my life. But it wasn't my gift. Even though people said I seemed at ease in front of an audience, I really wasn't. I had trained myself to appear at ease, and

that's a different thing. God had given me the gifts of administration and working with small groups, and I knew that was what I should be doing. I shouldn't be flying around the country, repeating words whose meaning I had only begun to understand. . . ."

Magruder was on to something vague and disconcerting about the born-again wardrobe that so many seem to seek while forgetting the perfectly good outfit they are at present wearing. I mean to say, is it absolutely necessary that we fall into the snare that confronted the farmer who saw a dazzling, angelic vision, the initials lighting up the sky with two magnificent letters: P. C. In pondering the initials, he told a friend that it must mean he could sell his farm, disperse his responsibilities, and Preach Christ. His friend, knowledgeable and saintly—and a true friend—replied, "No, perhaps it means more vividly, Plow Corn." Magruder is pursuing both. He notes that he will soon enter Princeton Seminary to follow a course leading to a master of divinity degree as preparation for the gospel ministry and ordination. Simultaneously, he hopes to enroll in neighboring Rutgers and gain a degree in their program leading to a master's degree in social work. He argues that he wants to keep his options open—either the ministry of the church or into secular work as a therapist, with a counseling practice. "I want," he writes, "to become involved with human need on a personal level."

Colson, Cleaver, and Magruder have all served different segments of time in prison. Cleaver is really the professional with a minimum sentence of fourteen years. He is not yet comfortable in pursuing a massive behind-the-bars crusade—but he is interested in dealing with the preventive forces that may keep young people out.

Magruder does not wish to pursue a prison ministry either, for reasons that are given in his writings. Colson, the

attorney, sees the conversion of convicts as a special
calling as well as being sensitive and alert to the particular problems of a prison society. There are 250,000 people
in prison in North America today. Colson has his work cut
out, but we must not forget the thousands of Christians
who were involved in this work before Chuck started
serving time and raising his sensitivity to their plight. It
might be time for the Christian community at large to
take the Reformation notion of the "priesthood of all
believers" seriously enough to regulate the excess enthusiasm over every new born-again experience. Just the fact
that a new convert feels an urge to suddenly start a massive new program does not necessarily call for support. In
fact, this urge may simply cause a fresh duplication of
effort and therefore create a further drain on Christian resources.

We forget that Calvin, with all his ecclesiastical brilliance and obvious religious motivation, always preferred
to be regarded as a layman. Calvin wrote four centuries
ago "that God, by a sudden conversion, tamed and made
teachable my mind." And in that teaching Calvin would
reshape the Reformed tradition of Christendom. These
bright moments of truth about God and His revelation
did not alter so much his life as to intensify his already
abundant talents. (It's interesting that Calvin could see
the whole picture, the blend of secular and sacred, the
holy and the profane. One of the essential changes he
brought to Geneva was not only the recapturing of the vitality of the Scriptures and its centrality in the Christian
life, but he also introduced dentists and street sweepers to
the Swiss metropolis. God uses our brains, our emotions,
our ecstatic surges for a variety of applications and pur-
poses. We must be prepared to sharpen our imagina-
tions.)

As we think about the coalition that gathers within the Christian fellowship—the combining of individual enthusiasm with institutional structures—we see many possibilities for the wider and healthier development of our society. Everything that I have read so far about born-again people keeps pointing to their desire to change the world around them as well as the world within. This is natural and valid. It is especially powerful when you consider the alternative described by William L. Shirer in *Midcentury Journey*. In 1950 he had returned from Europe to the United States to offer his appraisal of the decline of Western civilization. For him, and others, the decay seemed to have had a special residency in France. Something had happened to the French spirit, to the very soul of an historic people that brought them to such terrible collapse when Hitler knocked on their borders.

The American reporter quotes the French poet, Paul Valéry, as one source with knowledge and insight:

> The storm has ended, yet we are still restless and full of care. . . . We are aware that the charm of life and its abundance are behind us. . . . There is no thinking man who can hope to master this concern, or avoid the darkness. . . . All the foundations of our world have been shaken. . . . Something more essential has worn out than the replaceable parts of a machine. . . .

In *Flight to Arras*, that distinguished airman and patriot, Antoine de Saint-Exupéry, also cited the same circling doom when he wrote of his people,

> If the civilization to which I belong was brought low by the incapacity of individuals, then my question must be, "Why did my civilization not create a different type of individual? . . ." There was a time when my civilization proved its worth . . . when it enflamed apostles, cast

down the cruel, freed peoples enslaved . . . though today it can neither exalt or convert. If what I seek is to dig down to the root of the many causes of my defeat, if my ambition is to be born anew, I must begin by recovering the animating power of my civilization which has become lost."

In pondering these statements, I was led to think about Kenneth Chafin and his South Main Baptist Church in Houston, Texas. I also remembered the same sort of urban Christian work taking place with First Baptist of San Antonio and First Baptist, a neighboring congregation in Albuquerque. In his book, *Is There a Family in the House?* Chafin writes,

> The Church I pastor has 7,000 members and its buildings are located just off the downtown area in a transitional community. The location isn't good, the buildings are old, and the parking situation desperate. In spite of all these, the church is flourishing and the membership growing.

Chafin points to several reasons for this religious renaissance, not the least the spiritual reawakening of *families*—young families that are gaining a support and love and fellowship from church groups. People care about their being there, are in touch when absences occur, make provision for their children, and cast all of this in a healthy, happy social experience.

The second aspect of resurgence is the value of the whole family of God. People find in these downtown centers of Christ a place of belonging and love, a source of forgiveness and reconciliation that comes from God. In short, they are finding life, life in the spirit and life from which a civilization can gain purpose and direction. But it can only appear when individuals bring their faith into human affairs.

Maybe it ought to be considered that a born-again experience is a fresh start in what we are already trained to do. What's wrong with that? Mahalia Jackson reached as many, if not more, with her gospel concerts than if she had decided to be a full-time black woman preacher. Mark Hatfield, says Billy Graham, is practically a minister. Yet Hatfield's great ministry as a public servant and a U.S. senator has done far more than a thousand preachers in his faithfulness to speak on tough, difficult issues and to bring significant influence to the political arena he knows so well. (Hatfield, like Louie Evans, was one of the shaping persons in the development of Jeb Magruder. He also brought personal support to Chuck Colson during the formative stages of his Christian change.)

Right here I'm thinking about a friend's lay ministry. Let's call him Frank Wheeler (not his real name). For a significant time in his young adult and adult life, he exemplified the *Playboy* personality. The pursuit of fast cars and faster girls was a daily indulgence. His resources were ample, always sufficient to match his selfish style of existence. His parents were concerned Christians, but their influence seemed to melt when trying to lead Frank away from this determined, destructive behavior. Rebellious toward his family, he was incapable of responding to the call of the Gospel.

Within a short period of time both parents died. Frank suddenly found himself without family or any close relatives. As he sat in the church in preparation for his mother's funeral, he sensed that not only had her presence and love slipped away, but generations of Christian commitment were about to vanish. This heritage had been spiritually and morally committed. He was the last surviving member, and he was—nothing. This self-awareness increased. The goals and ethics of his life appeared worthless and empty. He was surrounded with a feeling of shame and sickened by the knowledge of this relentless self-indulgence.

The Sunday following his mother's burial, he quietly dressed and drove himself to the church of his baptism. Again, he sat in the pew and prepared for worship. He opened a Bible in the rack before him. The inscription on the front leaf said simply that this book was a memorial gift, presented by his own father. Tears welled up in Frank's eyes as he felt not only the depth and sincerity of his father's piety, but also the moving of God's spirit to bring him personally to the truth of Christ. Since that day seven years ago, Frank has pursued a discipline of daily prayer and reading of Scriptures.

Slowly and steadily the *Playboy* image evaporated and acts of kindness and caring have surfaced through his business activities. Known as a successful antique dealer, he travels widely to buy and sell and trade articles from the past. Often his visits take him to people who are desperate for cash and hopeful of his purchasing their possessions. Not infrequently Frank will gently lead the discussion beyond an immediate sale into the heartaches and sorrows that have created this crises—and bring out his own story about the love and grace of God. In at least two instances lately, he has been the agent to prevent suicide. For others, he has brought the gift of a Bible or some new translation of the Gospels. His own approach is to let others see what Christ can do—especially when misery and sin and selfishness seem so absolute, so unyielding. In his own congregation, he might be regarded as simply a faithful, thoughtful usher. But to the public beyond, the street people, the tormented couple on the edge of breakdown and collapse, he is ushering in fresh sensations of the Kingdom of God.

The appearance and growth of new religious organizations mean that the matters of the soul are primary to many people, that the particular spiritual objectives of a man or woman are knowing and following. Most of our present-day denominations in Christianity have come from the personality of a single individual caught up in the love of God and the persuasion of Jesus Christ—true, also, about the Catholic orders. The institutional effects of this are obvious as we have earlier discussed. Unfortunately, without renewal and reworking, these Christian organizations can lose their punch, misplay their vision, and become terribly self-serving to those in charge of the resources. Maybe we should follow Thomas Jefferson in this issue; he proposed, in secular arrangements, that the government ought to pay up its financial obligations during the lifetime of the generation that incurred them. He did not want future generations burdened with the indebtedness of the past—a marvelous idea, indeed! One generation did not have the right to bind another, he wrote in a letter to Madison. After thirty-four years, the books should be cleaned up. Then, he felt, this was too long for the big spenders and settled on ninteen years. I suggest that twenty-five years should be the time limit for a nonprofit organization to have a meaningful charter —then it should be forced to study and renew applications. Then we can see if these are viable Christian orders or tax shelters run by bankers.

We should swiftly admit that there is a difference between a worshipping community of believers and a nonprofit agency set up to do good works. In his new book, *Why Churches Should Not Pay Taxes*, Dean Kelley marshals some powerful arguments for his theme. He notes that tax exemption does not mean subsidy for congregations nor does it create money for their operations. Members provide the energy, love, and cash to make churches viable. One of his most telling points is the following:

> Churches provide a service or function that is essential to society as a whole and that tax exemption is an optimal arrangement for enabling them to do so.

7

New Faith—
New Fellowship

Jesus warned that you could not put new wine into
old wineskins—the ferment would burst the dry,
rigid leathers. So it is with our faith: we must have
resilient and expansive societies for an explosive,
exhilarating life in the Spirit.

KEEPING THE CONVERSION GOING, KEEPING THE FAITH ALIVE.

One of the major bewilderments for the Christian church today is how to keep the enthusiasm of a religious experience growing and expanding. Many traditional churches are frankly bewildered when a new Christian arrives, filled with joy and excitement over a fresh encounter with God through Christ. Too often established Christian groups have settled into formal patterns of study and worship, of service and outreach. The reawakened personality may have rejected these established forms and seek to develop more zestful and innovative expressions of caring. Jesus warned that you could not put new wine into old wineskins—the ferment would burst the dry, rigid leathers. So it is with our faith: we must have resilient and expansive societies for an explosive and exhilarating life in the Spirit.

Fortunately for us, there were few problems today that the first Christians did not face two thousand years ago. The conflicts over healing, speaking in tongues, authority in the church, and, yes, keeping the faith alive were just as current in the first century as they are in the twentieth.

Paul deals with this in a specific personal, meaningful way when he wrote to the Romans:

Do not be conformed to this world but be transformed by the renewal of your mind, that you may prove what is the will of God, what is good and acceptable and perfect [will of God.] (Rom. 12:2)

Let's go back for a moment to the buildup of this particular message that is so essential to us now. Paul was writing to second-generation, even third-generation Christians. The Gospel had drawn people to Christ all over the Roman empire—some historians estimate that there were at least a hundred thousand Christians in Asia Minor alone at the time of this epistle. In the first several hundred words of the book of Romans, Paul has been summarizing the Christian claim as he wrote from his location in Corinth to the expanding group of Christians in the empire city. It was simple: The Christian Gospel is good news; it is powerful; it makes one safe and hopeful and it is personal. That message had now gathered believers all over the place and the surge of this dynamic fellowship was attracting the negative attention of top Roman officials, including Pliny the Younger who sent an official secular communication to the secretariat of the Emperor Trajan, revealing this breathless report: "The contagion of this superstition has spread not only in the cities but the rural districts as well." The emperor and his court felt challenged by these new followers of Jesus Christ and the momentum they sustained for more than fifty years was directed by Paul to the "renewal of your mind."

And that mental enrichment gave Christian believers a powerful sense of liberation, freedom, and unity that flowed from no other source but the love and Spirit of

God. We all know how strikingly the lower class, slaves, and peasants, responded to the Good News. And here was Paul, writing within the confines of a secular state, with its enforced worship of Caesar, the crushing burden of taxes, and set within a civilization that had a population of which nearly half were slave and another third liable for immediate military conscription. It was a tightly structured, oppressive world.

Paul himself is writing about the mind's renewal from downtown Corinth, a metropolis Greek in history and tradition and corrupt with the ancient practice of religion served by temple prostitutes—numbering about a thousand during the writing of this material. Everywhere Paul could observe the grillwork of the empire, the depravity of man's lust, the perversion of religion, and the repressiveness of racism and clan that saturated the world of the first century. The place from which he wrote and the people to whom he addressed those letters had a firsthand knowledge of all this junk, yet the Apostle daringly and confidently says, "Do not be conformed to this world but be transformed by the renewal of your mind." (Rom. 12:2)

The transforming fellowship was with Christ, and the words, teachings, example, and love of the Savior came through meditation, teaching, study, learning, and dialogue among Christians.

The larger secret may rest with another passage that Paul proclaims along this line in his letter to the Corinthians. A transformation is possible—and keeps the personal faith stirring and growing and sparkling—because, he says, we "can have the mind of Christ." That has to be one of the more audacious and staggering assumptions to offer anyone—and for any of us to believe. Believers can now have this invincible intellect that belonged to Jesus and by which God informed the world, through the personality of His Son. It means that you can gain a transforming and renewing intellect, helping you to penetrate the folly of this age and perceive the glory of God.

Mert Martin was thrown out of high school for drinking. His behavior and language—profanity most of the time—were advanced for his age. So was his skill in construction. Local business types were impressed with his savvy around tools and materials. Yet his aggressive misconduct was more than the principal could take.

Martin signed up in the Navy. While waiting for completion of Sea Bee School and overseas assignment, he sampled the servicemen's clubs on weekends. One Sunday night he drifted into a Christian Servicemen's Center. The directness and personal appeal of the speaker was compelling—afterward he was asked by a businessman if he wanted to have eternal life, have joy in being released from sin, and find fulfillment in the presence of Christ. Somehow Mert said that it was just what he wanted. He experienced immediate peace and assurance that he had become a child of God.

The process of growth and a changed life was not instantaneous, but one thing was immediate and surprising. Overnight he stopped swearing. He had grown up using profanity, vulgar language, sometimes trying to control it, but always failing. In that California night of inviting Christ into his life, Martin found that Christ was really in his life, doing that which he personally could not accomplish.

The following year he was stationed in the Pacific, with a long assignment in the Philippine Islands. There he would become associated with a Christian fellowship and begin a navigator correspondence course on the Bible, sent to him from Colorado. This evangelical fellowship

touched not only Martin's life with a deepening relationship to Christ, but gave him the skills and training to
become one of their international leaders. Later he would
conduct missions in Korea, Mexico, and Central America
and eventually be the Regional Director managing navigator staff persons. The mind and the heart had been
transformed.

Now, as then, people must return to the power of their
mind, its renewing and regenerative strength, for there
God does meet us and lead us to the next vista of our
faith. Without the fresh consequence of Bible study and
discussion with other Christians, our whole structure of
belief starts to atrophy and we become candidates for the
style of religion that borders on being lifeless and pointless as well. Leslie Weatherhead, a British preacher,
shook his head sadly at those thousands of faded
members in his congregation and commented that, "unwilling utterly to surrender, they make do with religion
which is not Christianity at all, which uses the jargon
without the reality, the form without fire." It can happen
to anyone.

A new believer, a today convert, a born-again Christian
will only sustain his or her glowing faith through individual determination and the support of a sustaining fellowship. There is no other formula and no secret entry that
exists or works.

While we spend a lot of our life's energy gaining freedom and independence as persons, it is a true dichotomy
that only as we recognize our dependence on others in
the matters of faith and its development, do we approach
maturity as Christians.

Take Charles Lindbergh as an example. He crossed the
Atlantic Ocean alone, the first time in world history. Yet
everything about his solitary flight in *The Spirit of St.*

Louis pointed to his trust and faith in others. The design
of his aircraft, the dependability of his engine and equipment, the nervy band of investors from St. Louis—all
came together in a harmonious blend to make his flight
get off the ground. In his memoirs, Lindbergh freely ac-
knowledges his dependence and trust in others, while ad-
mitting that there were some things he had to do for himself, if ever he should fly.

For one thing, Charles Lindbergh had to gather all his
resources, including his life's savings, to make the enterprise work. Long before that moment, when as a youngster he slept on the back porch of his farm home in Min-
nesota, he would look out at the starry night and believe
that one day he would learn to fly through those heavens.

A most practical first beginning was overcoming his
fear of heights. So one shaky summer afternoon, he
climbed the village water tower to the very top, forcing
himself to accept the trembling panic, knowing that he
would go far higher than this when a plane left the
ground. His life, successfully and triumphantly, was a
grand alliance of self-assertion and dependence, fierce
pride and initiative, complete with barnstorming heroics
linked with the willingness to ask others for ideas, help,
cash, and backing. I cannot believe that the Christian enterprise is any different. Every person involved has to exercise individual responsibility regarding the matters of
faith and purpose. God gives us freedom to choose, a
world to inhabit, a life to fulfill, and a human endeavor to
enjoy. Always just ahead of us is that mad assortment of
options, choices, and variables that tells us we have a full
free measure of present existence. Yet Christians believe
that God is not passive, removed, distant, nor aloof. For
as Peter writes, "Blessed be the God and Father of our
Lord Jesus Christ! By his great mercy we have been born

anew to a living hope through the resurrection of Jesus
Christ." (1 Pet. 1:3)

Christians assert daily that what we know most fully
and lovingly about God has come through the life and
teaching of his Son. This does not sink in on one afternoon or a single inspiring laity conference in the mountains or along the shore. It more often is a process, a
steady development, an increasing awareness to the truth.
Christians also have come to believe that the love and justice and power of God is most adequately expressed in
classic terminology: Father, Son, and Holy Spirit. These
are names, terms, personalities that we are comfortable
with, for they happen to be human terms that are employed to describe divinity. They are still inadequate, for
we are creatures, the handiwork of God, yet we have
been assigned the gift of language, the processes of
thought, the intricate procedures of the heart. So from
very early days Christian folk have been led to use Father, Son, and Holy Spirit as manifestations of One who
made us and the universe.

There are additional realities, however, that God
chooses to reveal his ways, his personality, his arrangement, his plan, his grand design. And even with the most
saintly yearnings we are still, in the words of St. Paul,
people who see through a glass darkly. So God offers
three other realities besides Father, Son, and Holy Spirit—
he gives us faith, hope, and love. The born-again person
finds his or her world expanding through the positive
forces of these religious attributes.

When I entered the publishing field in 1964, I met several of the pioneer people in the great industry of books,
magazines, and periodicals. Television was making giant
steps in communication, and magazine publishers especially were feeling the heat of this awesome market rival.
Like people in other industries—cattle, energy, sports,

construction—publishers got together to discuss problems and share ideas for the solution of their mutual difficulties. During the decade that followed, I had the opportunity to meet and know David Lawrence of *U.S. News and World Report*, Henry Luce of *Time-Life-Fortune* fame, and Norman Cousins of *The Saturday Review* and, for a time, *McCall's*.

All were significant and fascinating personalities, but as circumstances and interests developed, I happened to become better acquainted with Mr. Cousins as I did several articles and features for *The Saturday Review*. My memory is somewhat vague, but I do recall that Jim Fixx mentioned that Cousins was convalescing from a severe illness that had lingered almost a year. All kinds of rumors had circulated, but since I happened to meet him on the health get-well side of his malady, our conversations never centered on his physical well-being. He chose to keep his personal situation private and nondiscussable; that is, until almost ten years later an article appeared in the *New England Journal of Medicine* in 1977, with further remarks in *The Saturday Review*, amplifying the editor's amazing recovery. In swift condensation this is what happened: Mr. Cousins returned from a European trip in August of 1964 with a slight fever. His limbs ached and he shortly learned that he was suffering from a rare case of spinal arthritis—the connective tissues of his spine were disintegrating.

Specialists were summoned, he could no longer turn over, raise his arms, his jaws were nearly closed, nodules appeared all over his body. And the most optimistic of his counselors said he had one chance in five hundred of not being an invalid the rest of his days.

Tragically, Cousins reacted violently to all attempts of prescribed treatment, finally, on his own, ordering that everything be stopped. He chose the pain to the prescriptions. And then, marshaling what energy and force remained, he recalled a book by Hans Selye, *The Stress of Life,* in which the argument is proposed that negative emotions and thoughts have a negative effect on body chemistry. Dr. Selye had shown that adrenal exhaustion could be caused by emotional tension, frustration, or suppressed rage. Well, Cousins admitted that his trip to Russia had created all those sensations, and everyone around him admitted that his adrenal glands were not doing anything to help Norman. Probably wore them out in dealing with the Russian scene.

Cousins did not quite become his own physician, but he did take dramatic action from that bed-of-iron confinement—he decided he needed sleep, so he rented a hotel room and moved from the hospital. He always trusted in Vitamin C so he started building up massive doses in place of twenty-six aspirin pills a day. Then he started his private nurses on a schedule of reading to him amusing, humorous books. Allen Funt sent over old films of hilarious scenes from "Candid Camera." Cousins noted that the more he laughed the less it hurt. His staff refused to permit anyone around him who was depressed or in a hand-wringing mood, or bearing solemn, somber ideas. Doctors discovered that the patient's blood chemistry was improving, especially after the long sessions of laughter and amusement. Even while he was hurting, he hurt less.

Cousins was really approaching a great truth of Creation, when he asked the question: Is it possible that love, hope, faith, laughter, confidence—and the will to live—have therapeutic value?

His answer was yes. He remarked in a May 1977 issue of *Saturday Review,*

> I did not accept the verdict, I wasn't trapped in the cycle
> of fear, depression, and panic—deep down I knew I had

a good chance and relished the idea of bucking the odds. Something else I have learned—to never underestimate the capacity of the human mind and body to regenerate —even when the prospects seem most wretched. The life force may be the least understood force on earth.

Faith, hope, love, and laughter—essentials to the living through these days. But how powerfully the New Testament enlarges on that formula, giving it a heavenly, God-like quality that far exceeds the ingenuity or improvisation of men and women.

By God's great mercy we have been born anew to a living hope through the Resurrection of Jesus Christ, and that continues as a gift of reality of God. And the Resurrection of Jesus headlines the relational factors of the Holy Spirit that followed and God the Father who sustains and creates in us life.

THE CHEMISTRY OF CONVERSION

Jesus was right: "The wind blows where it will, and you hear the sound of it, but you do not know whence it comes or whither it goes; so it is with everyone born of the Spirit." (John 3:8)

The factors that spark conversion are most varied and diverse. Some people are greatly moved by powerful preaching. When you study the life of John Wesley and examine the record of reaching so many persons with a life-changing message, you must admit a certain similarity to the conversions that took place. Historians claim that the common people in England had become so distant from organized Christianity that it required someone to go to them and be open, honest, and compelling. Such was Wesley. His piercing truth-filled messages had the energy to put listeners into convulsions—not of laughter, but of regret, shame, and repentance. The history of evangelistic preaching does have a responsive style associated with it. It was true of Charles Finney's preaching a century ago, and it is true of the Graham Crusades in the twentieth century.

A surprising number of individuals account for their born-again moment through the agency of a television appeal. I have known at least three middle-aged men who have recommitted their lives to Christ while sitting alone, at home, watching a Graham Crusade and making a silent, determined resolve in their own hearts. So the effect of mass psychology cannot be traced in such instances, including the obvious pressures from a surrounding, eager audience.

The born-again agenda takes many shapes and forms. It seems to have a certain holy chemistry that sparks conversion when the conditions are receptive and open. It may be a healing event, and it may precede such a recovery, prompted by the trials of life.

Victor Jameson, editor of the Presbyterian newsletter *Missionscope,* reported in his February 1978 issue that several years ago Charles Parvin, an editor with the *Chicago Tribune,* and his wife, Debbie, gave up their plush home in suburban Arlington Heights, Illinois, and volunteered for missionary duties for a year in Seoul, South Korea. Chuck taught journalism at a major university, and Debbie gave therapy to handicapped children in an urban hospital. Other interests included teaching Bible classes as well as circulating to other Christian projects in South Korea.

The motivation for this overseas spiritual investment is unique—it was the Parvins' way of giving thanks to God for the miraculous recovery that Debbie experienced in

1972 from a degenerative, terminal disease (closely related to muscular dystrophy). When Mrs. Parvin was thirty, with her own professional studio of voice and dance, she was suddenly paralyzed with this disability. For the following fourteen years, she experienced constant pain, was confined to a wheelchair, and according to Vic Jameson, frequently hospitalized.

Then during a November evening in 1972, when her energy and direction seemed finished, Debbie told her family and friends that she had a vision of Jesus Christ. Following this event, her condition improved. Physicians were puzzled by her sudden change. Tests of every kind were performed, and she was pronounced cured. More than that, her known heart damage, an ulcer, and a hernia were miraculously healed. Two years later, she gave up her wheelchair, is now a vibrant, dynamic Christian, able to give a full year to the rigors of overseas mission. She was born again, physically, emotionally, mentally, and spiritually and offers her life in thanks to Jesus Christ.

Or again there is the example of Alexander Solzhenitsyn who in the despair and the depression of the Soviet labor camp, surrounded by death and disease, came to the reality of the living Christ. What were the factors, what were the special agents, of his coming to the reality of God in Christ? A Pentecostal roommate, a phrase from Tolstoy, a remembrance from Dostoevsky, a flashing insight from the New Testament, a residue sensation, indistinct yet present, from the Orthodox Church. These sparks turned into glow and the glow flamed into a torchlight quality that lights up the sky in Solzhenitsyn's "Prayer":

> How easy it is for me to live with You, Lord!
> How easy for me to believe in You.

Solzhenitsyn had found the martyr's certainty, the saint's abiding satisfaction in the presence of God. He flatly stated that God had become a certainty—that not only did he exist but that he found servants to reflect his light to the world. He continues:

> To this point from which I can also reflect to men
> your radiance
> And all that I can still reflect—you shall grant to me.
> And what I shall fail you shall grant to others.

The circumstances of our existence vary so widely, so must the revelation of God in our lives. And as many have found, we are surprised by joy.

One must be amazed at the persistence and fortitude of people under such constant pressure, facing such steady opposition, and living with threatening surroundings. Our indebtedness is sometimes difficult to trace or accurately to interpret to others. William L. Shirer wrote movingly in *Berlin Diary,* his story of being a newspaper-radio correspondent in Nazi Germany prior to World War II. For three years he sent communiqués to America from downtown Berlin, then moved his headquarters to neutral Vienna in 1937. He observed how happy he was to be leaving Berlin and the thirty-six months of

> the shadow of Nazi fanaticism, sadism, persecution, regimentation, terror, brutality, suppression, militarism, and preparation for war which has hung over our lives like a brooding cloud which never clears.

Yet during this era of depression, riots, intimidation, and assassinations, he lists three things that held his personal world together in such menacing scenes: "Our refuge was our friends, our books, and ourselves." When you look at the famous and private conversion stories, it generally is that mixture over and over again. Colson leaning

on his friendship with Tom Phillips, a born-again businessman who gave him support and love; Malcolm Mug-
geridge turning to the Christian classic *Mere Christianity;*
Eldridge Cleaver helped by his own reading of the Scriptures, going again and again during the times of deepest
panic and regret to recapture the power of the 23rd Psalm
—plus the daring help of men and women like Art De
Moss and Floyd Thatcher, who took major risks to be
friends and helpers at every turn; Susan Atkins, one of the
convicted girls with Charles Manson, serving a life term
and finding a Bible in her cell and a belief that the Gospel
was meant for her, bringing love and liberation when all
over freedoms were gone forever.

Last winter I attended the dedicatory celebration of
the new community center for the Holy Trinity Greek Orthodox Church in Phoenix, Arizona. The master of ceremonies for the dinner event—which featured world Christian leader, Archbishop Iakavos—was Peter Kokalis. As
master of ceremonies, he was superb. He took time to recognize the many committees and individuals who made
possible this historic moment in the life of that southwestern congregation: planners, cooks, musicians, fund-
raisers. Then he stopped, put down his notes and said,

> Lastly, and most importantly, I want to thank Jesus
> Christ for what He has done for me. For His saving my
> life and giving me hope and confidence every day.

What I did not know, until later, was the information familiar to many within the audience—that Peter Kokalis
had experienced a miraculous, born-again healing experience following a terrible accident in the deepest Arizona
cave—the Black Abyss. In March of 1972 Peter had fallen
and, simultaneously, was crushed by a 5,000-pound boul-
der which fractured his right and left pelvis, broke his
back, crushed blood vessels in his lower back, and

inflicted possible damage to his spleen, liver, bladder, bowels, and pancreas.

Following an excruciating thirteen-hour trip to an Indian hospital at Tuba City, and then a flight to Doctor's Hospital, Phoenix, Kokalis faced a grim prognosis. Succeeding days brought no recovery, only further pain, inner anguish, a worsening condition. Death was, he felt, approaching. He called for the parish priest, Father James Tavlarides, to help him make his peace with God—an uneasy peace for a scientist who believed that God was dead and that most events surrounding his church life was a "humorous sideshow." Father Tavlarides brought two born-again Christians from the parish. Following the administration of the sacrament, the three laid hands upon the geologist's broken body and prayed for his recovery. Remembers Kokalis:

> What occurred next was not an emotional experience, certainly not an intellectual experience, and at the time not so much a spiritual event as an actual physical power that I can only describe as being similar to an electrical charge enter my body.

This physical sensation of power surged throughout his body, and it became so strong that Kokalis attempted to rise as he shouted, "I re-commit myself to Jesus Christ!"

From that moment Kokalis believed that he had received the "healing baptism of the Holy Spirit . . . I simply knew that I was healed." His marked improvement surprised the medical team which followed his case—many felt certain that he faced three to four years of rehabilitation and would probably never walk again.

Within seven months, wrote Kokalis,

> I put on my hiking boots and walked six miles on the mountain trails for the greater glory of God and to give living witness to His love for man.

He survived, he recovered, he lived—because Jesus Christ literally lived in him, hour by hour. "Finally, I want to thank Jesus Christ . . ."

Others are drawn to the Gospel through rather secular means: the vehicle of a stage play, the format of a modern film, the cutting edge of a television series. Sometimes a writer like Bergman introduces a thought-provoking, soul-searching revelation in the lives of his actors. In *Scenes from a Marriage,* Liv Ullmann and Erland Josephson portray a couple going through the pangs of divorce. Their family divides, the household separates, yet they continue to see each other from time to time. On one occasion of great candor, Erland blurts out with,

> We're taught everything about the body and about
>   agriculture in Madagascar,
> And about the square root of pi or whatever the hell
>   it is called—
> But not a word about the soul.
> We're left without a chance, ignorant and remorseful
>   among the ruins of our ambitions.

Other film makers have the capacity to create the stress and tension to cause people to confront the perplexities and moral dilemmas of human existence. When Italian film producer and director Federico Fellini was asked about his particular genius in shaping modern films with such powerful themes and ethical overtones, he replied that *if* he had such a talent or genius, it was his ability to leave an audience with "a deep sense of uneasiness." He argues that modern man does not have all the answers and even the best questions are poorly put.

Historian and English literature scholar Gilbert Highet once said that the Roman Empire finally changed and only changed when the Christian church created a sense of guilt and shame within the secular state. Such a saint as John Henry Cardinal Newman said that three distinct spiritual developments in his own life were caused by events outside of his normal existence—yet these forces created a stirring within his soul that gained a response which permanently affected his life.

The born-again experience currently enjoys an amazing amount of coverage in the media of Western civilization with a near-constant exposure in North America. For some people, it has a gee-whiz notion to it. What the general public does not know is how active and vigorous the born-again reality is in so many subcultures of our common life: southern mountain communities consider this reality part of a weekly religious celebration though not applicable to everyone who participates unless they are genuinely filled with the Spirit.

For others such as the black community in North America, the expression and vocabulary of the evangelical fervor is centuries old. It always has had a certain amount of mocking and put-down in plays and musical theater: a down home, darky, cotton field, lawdy-sakes, wide-eyed pickaninny description. To accept that parody is to miss the power and reach of a religious circuit that links millions of people.

Some human beings have lived so long and close to suffering, that religious interpretations and definitions of life are never far from the surface and the chemistry of conversion is everywhere at work. Mahalia Jackson, the renowned gospel concert artist, is an absolute illustration. She was able to give great exposure to the born-again belief through her vast and extensive series of appearances around the world. Much of her witness in concerts preceded by a decade the born-again phenomenon of the middle 1970s. While other entertainers might sprinkle their performances with references to God or appreci-

ation to the "Man Upstairs" for their talent, Jackson
would launch into a confession of faith in almost every
human encounter. Her relationship to Jesus and her trust
in God to help her get through the day was born out of a
humility and despair that surrounded so many black lives
for so many centuries. The daily theologizing that saturated her waking hours was not unique—or odd—to the
millions of other blacks who were going through the same
humiliation, the same replay of life-denying events in
human affairs. Jackson may have been unusual among entertainers in this regard, but not as a black woman raised
in dreadful neighborhoods and lifted up in the circles of
the black Christian community for her singing talent.

Jackson's art became the amphitheater for many of her
people and for the surging vitality of the Christian Gospel.
She sang and spoke and prayed with a universal appeal.
One of her most successful world tours included Japan.
Her Easter concert and the appearance for the emperor's
family at the Imperial Palace were history making in the
entertainment field. But Mahalia always, gently, firmly,
and occasionally vehemently praised God for her gift and
talent of song—to him belonged the glory.

When Japan's leading newspaper columnists reviewed
her performance at Tokyo's Bunkyo Kokaido, he confessed:

> Her first concert gave me so deep impression as I have
> never felt at any concert of classic, jazz, and popular
> singers. Her gospel songs have not only the perfect musi-
> cal beauty but also the persuasive power by her be-
> lief. . . . Though I am not a Christian, I could not stop
> running tears; tears of joy.

Others were to feel a different impact from the soul
singer, gospel star. When Mahalia decided to move to a
Chicago suburb in the early days of her career, the hostil-

ity and resentment of white Chatham Village flooded her with obscene letters and threatening telephone calls. She prayed, stuck to her convictions, and paid a doctor $40,000 cash for his attractive residence. While away on tour, violence erupted, and someone pumped bullets through her picture window. She persisted and returned home, with the FBI investigating. But her faith kept her well and determined. On the front door of her new home, after all the racket and rock throwing, she put up this simple sign:

DEAR LORD
IN THIS HOUSE YOU ARE WANTED
AND YOU ARE WELCOME.

When the Chicago black community winced at Martin Luther King's imprisonment in Birmingham, Alabama, and the black clergy of the Windy City were reluctant to sponsor a march and rally for the southern civil rights leader, Jackson stepped in. She personally gathered stars from radio, television, and the movies to put on a major fund-raising event that netted King $50,000 cash—all going for bail of civil rights activists.

Mahalia Jackson was once asked in a foreign press conference about the happiest moment in her life. She replied, "The only thing I could say, to me, is when I found favor in the sight of the Lord. Then, I felt happy. And this was not any big ovation, nor nothing; it was a quiet moment; and to me, in the solitude, by myself, being accepted as a Christian—I consider that the most happy moment in my life."

Several things are striking about the born-again experience as translated by Mahalia Jackson: The first is the natural ease in telling others, especially non-Christians, the depth and joy of her life in Christ. And just as important for her was the style of that conversion experience of becoming Christ's follower and sensing the certainty. It was a private, away from crowds, evangelists, and thunderous choirs. "It was a quiet moment, and to me, in the solitude."

There is every indication to assert this belief, that for every person who has the scintillating joy of a public profession of faith. There may be a dozen more who do not follow that particular religious style and discover the love and power of God in convincing, private, personal ways—and because of it, change the whole design of their lives. The mind has its reasons just as the heart has its verification. A Mahalia Jackson (like Jesse Jackson of today) brings a gospel message of practical application to her own people as well as to the general entertainment public that buys concert tickets. When invited to speak to black high schools in Los Angeles in 1962, she said,

I faced those young people and I talked about how you've got to help yourself do what you can if you expect help from other people. I stood there, a woman without formal education, who had made a name for herself through hard work and asking God's help every day. And none of those people could say a word back. There just wasn't anything to say.

Don't you know?

8

The Claims of the Cults and Response of Christians

Young people with great hopes and middle-aged persons with great misery are drawn into these extremist circles of religion, so desperate are individuals for a life of meaning, love, and purpose.

The born-again era lends glamour and excitement to a variety of new religious organizations, many of which are simply trading on the Christian currency. Some of the sect groups are entirely harmless, others are clearly sub-Christian and frequently anti-Christ. At the heart of almost every sect group parading to be within the Christian fellowship is a dominant, authoritarian director, leader, guru, what-have-you. The interpretation of Scripture, the daily rules and regulations, the formal observances and ecclesiastical protocol are entirely in the hands of this self-designated saint/seer.

Young people of impressionable age are drawn to such rigid and ruling power figures. Often their unresolved guilt—real or imagined—and their native idealism are enough to fuel a surging movement that may masquerade for a while with religious trappings and Christian-style vocabulary, but at the heart is a distorted person seducing believers away from Jesus Christ.

You know the names of these groups. I prefer not to mention them here, for I am tired of their harassing phone calls, their threatening letters, their intimidating innuendos. For more than a decade I covered the events and personalities of the world religion scene in a weekly newspaper column syndicated to nearly six hundred newspapers in the United States and Canada. Invariably I would be targeted for mail abuse and telephone threats when even the slightest question was raised about the integrity or purpose or mission of these sect groups. They have become sick groups and the sickness is unto death, to quote Kierkegaard, for they border on an insane frenzy that parades as true and absolute Christianity—except for faith, hope, and love. The world, alas, is filled with Charles Mansons, plundering deserts with their mad visions, and innocent lives with their treacherous designs. And the alert and wary persons, Christian or not, must now recognize how many groups flourish with Christian vocabulary, the signs and symbols of the cup and the Cross, the wardrobe of collar and cloth, and are revealed, time and again, as the master agents of satanic service. Perhaps Christians should feel honored that their Lord is so frequently and faithfully copied, his ways and words counterfeited and duplicated. Perhaps it is the great power of the Faith that so many want to promote its promises and merchandise its glory. Let us warn and be warned by Paul who knew that "evil men and imposters will go on from bad to worse, deceivers and deceived." (2 Tim. 3:13)

Like most readers we all have suffered at the manipulations of the cults—the preposterous theological interpretations, the enticement of teen-agers into religious colonies that turn out to be outdoor prisons, the warped lives escaping to reclaim sanity and re-entry into American society. The lying. I believe that the fraudulent aspects of the current religious frenzy are as marvelous as the energy that it channels into an apocalyptic theater lived out by the believers. Tillich was so correct—no fraud is as bad as a religious fraud. The final game, the ultimate

crunch, from the manipulation of these masquerading
messiahs is the game of sex, money, and violence. Swiftly
these cults suck up all the resources of the new converts,
getting the cash value of their homes, cars, life insurance
policies, sports equipment, hi-fis—all the articles that prevent the new believers from finding ultimate "spiritu-
ality."

Then the switch—to labor on farms and ranches and ag-
ricultural communes and even warehouses, motels, and
restaurants for the spiritual Hitler who runs the whole
show. All in the name of God or Jesus or the faith—whatever the words that enforce the designs of the inner circle, who eventually use sex, physical intimidation, and
group control to achieve their heretical goals. Young people with great hopes and middle-aged persons with great
misery are drawn into these extremist circles of religion,
so desperate are the individuals for a life of meaning,
love, and purpose. Those high aspirations of the true
Christian life, with its golden fellowship and redeeming
love—all that is the front advertisement of the cults that
storm across America. A sense of adventure, daring, and
risk have an intoxicating aroma for the new born, the converts to the cults. Some newcomers are burned out on
drugs, others have suffered from white slavery and prosti-
tution and child pornography, and the absolute claims of
the new religious cults seem so right and helpful and
timely. Anything, anywhere, just to find the inner balance
and the hope for a heart which has gone without so
long . . .

People struggling for a genuine Christian expression
must be warned constantly about the perils of spiritual se-
duction. When a person is attracted to whatever group,
name, or organization that proposes Christian formulas of
salvation and recovery, let them be warned and cautious,

especially when they offer to surround you with club members who bring housing and food and shelter. Most cults will not let you go home at night, be with your friends, contact your family. It is for your own good, they say, if you truly believe, you must validate that conviction by giving up family, friends, and present surroundings, so they say. When you accept this, it is good-by and you will need more than good luck to come out whole again.

The cultic religious danger was first flashed by the Manson murders in California. Since the initial group was so small and made up finally of fewer than a dozen wayward young women, the public dismissed this as some weird desert clutch of mindless hippies lost in their own dementia.

But the warning signals have persisted. Religious cults seemed to flourish in the South and West, building on the attractions of an outdoor, low-income, low-profile experience. The fluid state of society in California would be the ultimate assembly grounds for many of the larger, more outrageous groups, culminating in the Peoples Temple of San Francisco, headed by the Reverend Jim Jones. This cultic leader was persuasively able to direct the mass suicide and slaughter of more than nine hundred followers who were residents of the Jonestown complex in Guyana, South America. At last the whole world would see the wretched, sick behavior of a religious cult that masqueraded as Christian and followed a gospel of death in place of the good news of Christ.

RESPONSE TO THE CULTS

Christians with real caring for young people will want to study carefully the research compiled on the Unification Church, a heretical body if there ever was one. This international cultic organization directed by Reverend Sun Myung Moon is moving forward with the zeal and motivation of early Christians. Indeed, Barbara Hargrove, associate professor of sociology of religion at Yale Divinity School, says that the Christian community may want to give this movement far more credit for genuine religious expression than previously acknowledged.

Ms. Hargrove spent considerable time visiting the Moon training centers and interviewing new recruits converted to the Unification cause. She argues that its influence is not based on brainwashing, nor even on the restriction of personal movement of the new members. (While this may happen in individual cases, it does not seem to be a generally enforced maneuver to keep converts loyal to the cause.) Rather, Hargrove argues, the success of the Moon movement as a viable religious force is traced to five distinct realities. In her essay "Some Advice for the Moon-Struck," which appeared in the April 1978 issue of *Reflection* published by the Yale Divinity School, Hargrove elaborates on these points. One key is *fellowship:* every new member sincerely believes that the Moon group cares about him or her individually and personally. In a world where college campuses have become frightfully impersonal and where secular society seems bent on dehumanization, these new members thrive on the loving, caring, personal attention showered on them by the Moon cadre.

Another basic rule is *participation:* every member of this religious group participates actively through the local church unit. Although terribly autocratic at the national level, there is a surprising amount of input and planning by the local members—almost all of whom are young and involved. Thus the feeling of self-determination flourishes —even within a very rigid over-all system.

Another factor is *commitment:* young people who link up with Moon must take the big plunge and commit their lives absolutely to this brand of religion. Many had been lost in the permissiveness of society and the vagueness and indifference of adult standards in the home. Rampant divorce, family disintegration, urban chaos—all become the urgent reasons for a youngster to willingly and devotedly sign up with intense commitment that they now perceive as a saving experience.

Christian education is paramount. Countless young people have no connection or grasp of the Bible or no formal religious training. They suffer from a great intellectual/spiritual vacuum concerning matters of the spirit. The Moon style of indoctrination and teaching is total and, frequently, tiring. Long lectures and saturated reading assignments fill up the day. Yet these young people seem to thrive on this since they are gaining for the first time a theology and religious doctrine that makes sense to their future. To traditional Christians, it smacks of heresy, from top to bottom. But to these new believers, it is the bread and water of life to a starving pilgrim.

Relevance is the final key. Moonies believe that they are in touch with a worldview that is winning. Their efforts are linked with a holy plan of God to bring the world to judgment and justice. They see history coming to a grand finale with the Second Coming of Christ right away. They believe that international order, through economic justice, world law, and the end of starvation, war, and misery will soon come to pass. What they are doing addresses the immediate anl specific heartaches of humanity. And who doesn't want his or her life to be both relevant and successful?

Hargrove concludes that the Moon movement would never have surfaced had the world Christian community been living up to its own established goals and great vi-

sion of Christ. Born-again believers would say that in
their experience, they have discovered *all* the five principles so vigorously advertised by the Moon heresy. If that
is true, then we can look for new advances to emerge
from the current religious enthusiasm generated by the
thousands who are responding to the claims and joys of
the Gospel.

Already we have seen some of the significant strengths
of the born-again phenomena. Joseph Fichter, writing in
the March 17, 1978 issue of *Commonweal,* developed a
long and thoughtful essay on the events surrounding the
present revival in America. While disagreeing on some of
the theological points that always tend to divide lib-
eral/conservative Christians, Fichter identified the real
power of contemporary American revivalists:

> They show a loving concern for their neighbor who is in
> trouble. Part of their attractiveness is that they offer love
> and solace to the confused and alienated people of our
> society. The corporal works of mercy, feeding the hungry,
> caring for the sick, comforting the elderly, are manifes-
> tations of their service to the Lord through their service
> to his children. It may well be that this human warmth of
> a personal kind is a more powerful force for conversion
> than is their set of simple religious beliefs.

Whether these doctrines—the inspiration of the Holy
Spirit, an infallible Bible, the Virgin Birth, the Atonement
of Jesus, the Second Coming—are simple or profound,
they are unquestionably the most powerful factors that
have stirred through Christianity for the past four centuries. In our own era, they appear to be the driving force
behind several social movements that shape the Christian
development in secular society.

Much of the recent controversy over the effectiveness
of the born-again believer centers around the style and

expression of Christian ethics. Faith is not the point of difference, rather it is the ethical translation of this new religious experience into the life stream of the world. Christians have always enjoyed a spirited discussion over the application of the gospel—or nonapplication, if you will. Social activists, reformers, even revolutionaries have contended that without a serious attempt to put the values of faith into everyday events, it is worthless and fraudulent. Others have believed that only as others have learned the primacy of a personal faith, will the subsequent expression be worth noting.

Criminals and prison reform, homosexuality: sickness or sin?, world hunger, ghetto life, the drug culture—all are topics that evoke a variety of responses by Christians today. The born-again community has only marginal confidence in the glorious claims of the fading Great Society blueprint of government to solve social problems. Indeed, conservative Christians are among those who raise the largest questions concerning the efficacy of federal programs or the master plans of politicians for meaningful social change.

Within the church, the real stress comes from those who would shift secular goals onto the agenda of congregations. Political solutions to spiritual problems do not attract increasing excitement. At present the World Council of Churches is in deep water, up to its armpits, for making substantial grants to black revolutionary groups in Africa—who in turn have been charged with the murder of white missionaries. In America, Christians have been sharply divided over the effectiveness of gaining social justice through boycott programs against growers, manufacturers, and mill operators. But the biggest brawl lately was the church's consideration of homosexuality.

The thrust of gay liberation groups began in the early sixties to gain approval and acceptance in the mainstream of American society. By 1973 several homosexual advocacy groups had announced joint meetings with the Nomenclature Committee of the America Psychiatric Association—a step to remove the term "homosexual" from the diagnostic manual and purge the term from the realm of psychiatry.

By the end of that year it was announced in a joint news conference—the National Gay Task Force and the American Psychiatric Association—that the term homosexual would no longer be used and the condition no longer considered an illness.

Within the next two years, the major Christian denominations would be invited to study the reverse process that had been momentarily successful with the psychiatrists—to remove the condemnation of homosexuality as being a sin and to open the way for avowed homosexuals to be ordained to the Christian ministry. (This was not new. Homosexuals were active in the leadership of the Metropolitan Church across North American religious congregations, which openly espoused the gay rights cause and acknowledged that their pastors were homosexuals.)

Dr. Armand Nicholi, Jr., psychiatrist at Harvard Medical School, summarized the dilemma for Christians when he addressed several hundred delegates during the United Presbyterian Church General Assembly in San Diego, 1978.

> The Scriptures, it seems to me, leave us uninformed about many issues—but spell out clearly and explicitly the ones we need to know. The sexual ethic is certainly spelled out clearly in both the Old and New Testament documents.

Dr. Nicholi, an active Christian in the Boston community, admitted that society in general seemed to have

rejected biblical ethics and purchased a new permissiveness—which

> is not always what it's cracked up to be. If one speaks
> with many of the people caught up in this new freedom,
> it soon becomes clear that it seldom leads to ecstatic
> pleasure, to greater freedom and openness between sexes,
> to more meaningful relationships or to exhilarating relief
> from stifling inhibition. . . . Instead, it leads to turmoil
> and often to tragedy. It often leads to superficial, empty
> relationships that attempt to test one's masculinity or
> femininity: to feelings of guilt, of self-contempt, of
> worthlessness; to unwanted pregnancies—with hundreds
> of thousands of pregnancies now occurring in *children*
> and in very young teenagers."

The address of Dr. Nicholi to members of that national
church convention seemed to many observers to be the
turning point for Presbyterians as they measured the arguments for homosexual approval and ordination—and
found them inadequate. Although the wide Presbyterian
community had rejected the style and theology of Anita
Bryant, being people of the Bible, they still wanted to
affirm the truths of Scripture in their own time.

Drawing on his university practice, Dr. Nicholi noted
that many college students were now rejecting the new
morality and embracing the Christian faith because it did
propose clear-cut "boundaries imposed by Christian morality less confusing than no boundaries at all and helpful
in relating to members of the opposite sex as persons
rather than sexual objects."

In summarizing his view as a Christian psychiatrist, the
Harvard professor stated flatly,

> Homosexuality is a mental illness—to encourage homo-
> sexuality is to encourage extinction of the human race, for
> no society has or ever can accept or encourage homosex-

uality without sowing the seeds for its own destruction. . . . The church cannot endorse or approve in any way homosexual behavior if it's going to uphold the Judeo-Christian code and if it's going to fulfill its responsibilities to society.

9

Born Again and Again

Martin Niemöller, one of the distinguished and courageous churchmen in this century, wrote once that his
second conversion was the one that gave him the
whole glimpse of God's saving plan in Christ.

Those who have experienced a new resolution of life through a born-again experience often point to specific changes that continue to happen—suggesting that a spiritual revelation is not limited to one time or place but that it is possible to receive many such moments of truth. When you study the life of Simon Peter in the New Testament, you follow almost a series of spiritual revelations through the high and low encounters of his human existence. From the Mount of Transfiguration to the valley of denial—all are encounters and conflicts of decision. Even his vision of which food is clean and unclean as reported in Acts is still another revelatory moment of truth in his openness to the moving of the Holy Spirit.

Martin Niemöller, one of the distinguished and courageous churchmen of this century, wrote once that his "second conversion" was the one that gave him the whole glimpse of God's saving plan in Christ. Niemöller had been a tireless and vocal critic of Adolf Hitler and the Nazi regime. His sermons and radio broadcasts from his pulpit in Berlin irritated Hitler no end. Albert Speer wrote that Niemöller was one person who could send

Hitler into a frothing, foaming rage. Once too often, in 1937, the German pastor spoke out and Hitler sent him to a concentration camp.

While in confinement, Niemöller said that he could hardly regulate his bitterness and anger toward the fascist desecration of humanity. The arrogance, the atrocities, the inhuman behavior was overwhelming—and all of this anger he finally directed toward the prison guard who daily brought him his meals. Finally, it dawned upon Niemöller that God's grace was stronger even than his righteous anger—that Christ had died also for this sinner in a Nazi uniform. Only as he was able to pray for his enemies, specifically for his guards, did he arrive at a new level of the meaning of the Cross. Christ's love and sacrifice was unconditional, and Niemöller found in that truth his second conversion. He also found a will to live and survive.

In *Inside the Third Reich*, Albert Speer, the gifted young architect who would plan and design for the Third Reich, tells of seeing Reverend Niemöller. It was the day Speer entered the Allied prison camp and Niemöller, with others, was being released from seven years of incarceration. By chance, their groups were using the same large buses to move those liberated and to pick up those about to be tried and sentenced at Nuremberg. Said Speer,

> Word went around that Pastor Niemöller was among them. We did not know him personally, but among the new arrivals was a frail old man, white-haired and wearing a black suit. The designer Flettner, Heinkel and I agreed that he must be Niemöller. We felt great sympathy for this man so visibly marked by many years of concentration camp. Flettner took it upon himself to go over

to the broken man and express our sympathy. But no sooner addressed him than he was corrected—"Niemöller is standing over there." And there he stood, looking youthful and self-possessed—an extraordinary example of how the pressures of long imprisonment can be withstood. Later, I would think often about him.

Emerson was correct when he confided that rarely can we affect the great events but we can affect ourselves. Solzhenitsyn has one of his heroes reading the journal of his mother who urged upon her communist son a return to the values of truth, love, and justice. She added that one cannot prevent the massive evils that inflict the world, but you can do your best to prevent its capture of your own soul. We each must start with ourselves for it would be false and certain failure to believe that any effect can spring from an uncommitted life.

Dean Kelley, studying the forceful spiritual victories of the Anabaptists and the Wesleyans in his book *Why Conservative Churches Are Growing*, pointed to what he identified as the Power of the Gate. Five distinct habits were pervasive in the lives of these powerful Christian sects. As you ponder them, think how this applies to your own religious arrangements:

1. Be in no haste to admit members.
2. Test the readiness and preparation of would-be members.
3. Require continuing faithfulness.
4. Bear one another up in small groups.
5. Do not yield control to outsiders nor seek to accommodate to their expectations.

One recognizes here a certain hesitancy to receive new believers, a divine pause before flinging wide the gates of

belonging and support. Is that justified? Is it Christian?
Jesus said,

> Enter by the narrow gate; for the gate is wide and the
> way is easy, that leads to destruction, and those who
> enter it are many. For the gate is narrow and the way is
> hard, that leads to life, and those who find it are few.
> (Matt. 7:13–14)

Perhaps the fullness of the Gospel and the invitational
style of Jesus himself should be the final direction of this
recruitment and receiving of members. In 1978 George
Gallup, Jr., did a special study of the unchurched people
in America. Among other things, he learned that "half of
the unchurched said they could be brought back into the
church under certain conditions, such as finding clergy
they could confide in or a church that offered good
preaching and whose people were receptive." Gallup
noted that at least 25 per cent of the unchurched people
in America had experienced a profound born-again experience. There were clear indications that many people
were unchurched because they had never received a personal invitation to unite with a body of believers.

If invitation is going to lead to integration of new
believers into the broad mainstream of Christianity, certain distinct moves must develop in all the Christian communities that are truly open to the fresh arrivals. The attitudes, sentiments, and game plan of any such
development is going to be finally expressed by the men
and women in the pew. The up-front pronouncements
and the ecclesiastic proclamations of church bodies
means absolutely zilch unless the involvement of the laity
is real and working.

Several springs ago, Sen. Mark Hatfield invited me to
dinner at his Maryland home. We were visiting about

some projects of mutual concern and he also wanted me
to meet Chuck Colson who had newly arrived to the
Washington scene, fresh out of prison and zooming
around the country with a born-again theme. One cannot
avoid a certain bracing, building of prior defenses for
such an evening. The papers had been full of Colson's
conversion—and full of editorial disappointment that he
had not told more tales on Nixon and Company. His spi-
raling celebrity status was enhanced by his new prison
ministry. Now he was giving lectures, sermons, and inspi-
rational talks all over the place, sounding erudite in theology, social concern, and individual spiritual growth.

The evening was a pleasant surprise. Colson had no
agenda to sell the dinner party, no program for saving the
Christian world from chaos, no presumption that his
born-again experience had all the answers for everyone
struggling with the same large questions of the mystery
and joy of life. But one could appreciate the working of a
determined believer, a new Christian who had gone
through a total change and wanted the unfolding days
and months to yield growth, liberation from sin, and an
increasing response to the Spirit of God in Christ.

Aside from Colson's prison ministry, one was sensitive
to a big, creative mind that was applying a lot of brain
power to the puzzled and frustrating diversions that
afflicted contemporary Christianity. Since that first meeting, I have had the opportunity to hear Colson several
times, follow the direction of his thought, and weigh the
analysis of his approach to the current human scene.
What emerges is depth and what is produced is a new
view of an old dilemma: how to get Christians of
varying persuasions and theology into a viable encounter with the heartaches of the humanity.

Colson summarized these reflections in his article published in *Christianity Today* entitled "Religion Up, Morality Down" by saying that

Divisions within the body of Christ over theological, social, and structural issues too numerous to list here rob us of spiritual unity, hence of power. Many believers —some expecting the Lord's return any moment, others merely content with their own piety—seem to care only about rescuing lost souls. But personal holiness without social holiness is disobedience to Christ's second great commandment and a disembodying of the Gospel. . . .

Colson is anxious that we

have so accommodated the Gospel to twentieth-century humanism that what we offer is no more than a better way for man to achieve his humanistic goals—from personal gratification to nationalistic power.

Central to the Christian theme is the love and power of God in Jesus. Colson fears that we have translated that message to mean that

Christ will give you a more abundant life, the word *abundant* understood in this age of obsessive materialism to mean "the good things of life."

His other concern is that some Christians believe that

God has singled out America for his chosen purpose. . . . and [we] make the Gospel hostage to the political fortunes of a nation.

If our congregational life and our wider church affiliations are to have meaning and a cutting edge, we must go back again to the New Testament. "We must realize once again," said the Watergate plotter, "that the Church of Jesus Christ is not an evangelical fellowship club. It is a

holy nation, a royal priesthood, the very living presence
of God's rule here and now, the means through which
God brings about not mere revival but reformation."

If the born-again experience is to be a gateway—an entrance for thought and action and fellowship—then
specifics are in order. Colson offers seven pragmatic directions for persons serious about their faith:

1. *"Be an authentic witness to one other person."*
   Programs of individual Christian involvement—such as
   Michigan's Volunteers in Probation and California's
   M-2 have made a significant impact on the lives of former convicts. The point is not only to visit prisoners
   but persons in juvenile centers, nursing homes, and
   health centers.
2. *"Teach another to be a disciple."*
   Perhaps too much time is spent in broadcasting the
   good news and not enough follow up to live the good
   news. Christians need to be one to one in conversation
   and prayer, deepening the life of Christ within each
   other.
3. *"Get involved with moral issues."*
   In a society saturated with so many negative, anti-
   Christian forces, Christians can no longer remain on the
   sidelines. The leadership of Christians in public life
   should call forth our support and backing. The homosexual onslaught for approval—even ordination in the
   churches—requires a determined and vigorous response from the caring community of faith.
4. *"Encourage Bible study and biblical preaching."*
   As Gallup observed, many unchurched people would
   return to the fold if good preaching were a high priority of the church today. Biblical preaching must be
   central and incisive.
5. *"Urge your church to expand its vision."*
   More and more congregations are supporting mission in
   their neighborhood as well as in Africa. Concern for

housing, health, and human rights is not a government monopoly. Where there are people, there we must find the working of the good news as well as its proclamation.

6. *"Each day demonstrate the whole Gospel."*

Every believer can and should find daily spontaneous expression of his faith. This is literally world changing when millions of Christ's people start to respond to specific needs and opportunities.

7. *"Examine how much of your Christian effort involves genuine compassion."*

Christians cannot permit themselves to be cut out of the mainstream of the world's dilemmas. Great revivals historically have sponsored significant change on the human landscape. The shutting down of the slave trade, the public spectacle of executions, child labor laws, the clearing of slums, the closing of poor house and the debtor's prison, the care and treatment of drug addicts, and the whole realm of prison reform can be traced to Christian motivation at work in secular society. Opportunities abound today and the imagination of the mind and the compassion of the heart can be the result of a Christian conversion.

Jesus says that if we are to be workers in the vineyards of the Lord, laborers responding to the harvest that God has prepared, *it will be in relation to him and to each other*. Christians do not live and grow and worship in splendid isolation. Very few are smart enough or powerful enough for that solitary, saintly experience with God. They were a company of believers, and the moment that group convened, you have the original framework for the institutional church. For this was a place of prayer and instruction; a classroom of teaching; a gathered community for nourishment, encouragement, and inspiration. And if the new workers in the universe of God were to be at spe-

cial tasks, those would have to be identified and assigned.
Matthew has the work list that Christians have not only
memorized by memorialized in their work-worship since
New Testament days.

It became the hallmark of a living faith, the validation
point of Christian service—it was the work of Jesus Christ
and represented a working Father. In the twenty-fifth
chapter of Matthew:

> to tend the sick
> to feed the hungry
> to give drink to the thirsty
> to clothe the naked
> to harbor the stranger
> to minister to prisoners
> and to bury the dead.

And those classic commandments of love are fulfilled
most diligently today in the companionship and integrity
of *Christian people joined together.*

It must be clear to us that the most powerful and consistent expression of doing the works of God as seen in
Christ, *will be fulfilled in the energies of the wider fellowship.* One hastens to say that the personal, individual,
intimate, and inspired acts of mercy that Christian people
accomplish, hour by hour, particularly their prayers and
reaching out, is the hidden support system that makes a
living fellowship possible. It was true in Jesus' time, it
happened for St. Paul, and it is just as real today.

But we are advanced and sagacious enough to know
that much of the significant Christian enterprise in our
century is expressed through the *vitality and muscle of institutions.* When we see the great work of hospitals and
sanitariums, when we trace overseas witness to the Gospel
in foreign fields, when we observe the impact of Christian
colleges and seminaries, when we visit the vigorous mis-

sion outreach in our nearest neighborhoods, we can speak confidently and forcefully about the blessings of the institutional church of which we are a living part.

For Christians life is a blend of individual initiative and corporate consolation; it is a balance of personal persuasion and public worship; it is a holy formula of particular people belonging and uniting under a Provident Father. We can do nothing without the leading and directing and correcting of the Holy Spirit. And even inspired separately, we are fragmented and disappointed, until we are forged into one Holy, Living Fellowship of Jesus Christ. This is the source of our power, and this is the need, the absolute need. Nothing lasting will happen alone.

Several years ago I visited one of our sons in Children's Hospital, Buffalo, New York. He had just had a successful operation, and as I was driving out of the parking lot, I came up to an intersection and waited for the light to change. There, on the bench where people waited for the bus, was a small youngster, seven or eight years of age. His foot was bandaged. He was sitting alone and tears were streaming down his face. There was no way that I could drive on, so I called out and asked if he wanted a ride home—and he did.

When he got in, I asked him what was wrong. And he rubbed his eyes again, and his whole face was washed with tears. He had broken his ankle that summer—(he was a child of the ghetto) and the joint had been set, and it had healed. But they had just x-rayed his foot, and it had not healed correctly and now they were going to have to do the operation all over again. . . . And life was hard, and his mother had to work, and his father was gone, and he was waiting for the bus to go home and face the misery and emptiness and despair of that day.

As I thought about his recovery and his future, I knew

this much: that I could give him a lift that day and tell
him to buck up and things really would work out. But it
at last would be the loving care of Children's Hospital, an
institution, that would finally get him running and laugh-
ing again—his surgeon, the operating room staff, the floor
nurses, the attendants, the people in therapy, the cleaning
ladies and maintenance staff, the social workers, the char-
ity dollars. All this would come to pass, and that is how
things work out; and they function most beautifully when
people say: "I read in John 5:17 that Jesus said and promised, 'My Father is working still, and I am working.'"

Any understanding, definition, or elaboration of the
born-again movement within Christianity is going to be
provisional at best. We are living in a spiritually dynamic
moment, and we all have a unique opportunity to make
some special contribution to this holy hour. Over the
years one person has continued to stand out in my mind
as willing to share fully in the process of being a Christian
in the twentieth century—to enter into the renewal and
rejuvenation of the Spirit. Mark Hatfield has been a
friend and counselor to many old and new Christians—
including this writer. His statement of faith speaks for
many when he says in his book *Between a Rock and a
Hard Place,*

> If we are called to Christ, then our lives are to take on his
> shape. Whether teachers, doctors, businessmen, politi-
> cians, lawyers, laborers, or ministers, our first task is to
> embody the quality of Christ's life. Faithfulness to this
> call totally transcends any requirements of "success"
> posed by our vocations or the conformist opinions of soci-
> ety.
> Identified truly with Christ, we will find ourselves serving
> the oppressed of the world—the victims of injustice and
> sin . . . our hope rests in the promise of God's ongoing

love, and his intention to effect a new order in human affairs. This we first grasp among the people called to be the body of Christ. There we discover God's revolutionary act of pouring his life into others, who share in common God's Spirit. We see the hope of all things being renewed as this corporate life is given in sacrificial service for the world.

As Christians struggle with these questions, they find significant help and direction from new believers who have suffered through upheaval and catastrophes that afflict society. The clear, stark change of conversion brings hope to the individual and vitality to the church. Any assessment of the born-again surge in contemporary American life must recognize a new awareness of the crunching power of sin. For long years that word was regarded as quaint in secular society and had nearly become an embarrassment in some Christian circles. People spoke of failures, mistakes, and regrets—but rarely admitted of "sin."

Karl Menninger may have been the first to argue for a return to reality when he said in *Whatever Became of Sin,*

> We have called sin two things, a crime and lock people up who deviate. Or we call it mental illness and put people in mental hospitals. What about the bulk of the problem which is neither crime nor mental illness? This is man's willful, moral irresponsibility. Let's call it by it's right name. It's not a disease or a crime. It's sin, something deep in the heart of man that needs challenging.

Christianity has survived and extended its influence in human life by its inner corrective capacity—to examine its own method, to appraise its own message. At times it swings too far in one direction, pursuing logical goals to illogical ends. H. Richard Niebuhr recognized this among the social idealists who captivated the church for a while in the late nineteenth century.

The enthusiasm for social change was genuine and contagious. The programs and institutions that followed were strong and vital. But social work could never replace the Gospel, only distort its primary message of salvation with an agenda of good works without faith. Said Niebuhr:

A God without wrath, brought men without sin
  into a kingdom without judgment
    through the ministrations of a Christ without a Cross.

The Cross has become central again. The renovation of the Christian community is being staffed by many new converts, countless new believers, a host of born-again persons who want the full experience of Christ in their daily life. One day these hosts of new members will want a wider, richer, more expansive life in the Spirit. And the Christian church will be there, to offer its broad picture, its diversity and plurality, that everyone might know the fullness of the grace of God.